BRAVE IN RIBBONS

Brave in Ribbons

A
Transgender
Christmas Carol

Holly Maholm

ANGRY RABBIT ENTERPRISES LLC • CLEVELAND, OHIO

ISBN: 978-0-9818090-2-1

The trademark SCRABBLE used on page 23 of the text is a trademark of Hasbro, Inc.

The trademark FERRAGAMO used on page 51 of the text is a trademark of Salvatore Ferragamo S.P.A. of Florence, Italy.

Library of Congress Control Number: 2015908164

Published by Angry Rabbit Enterprises LLC located at 3550 Harvey Road, Cleveland Heights, Ohio 44118

Gratefully Acknowledged: Keith Witmer, Illustrator, of Portland, OR for illustrations and cover art; Stephen Tiano, Book Designer, of Calverton, NY for interior page design and layout; and Sheila Hart, Graphic Designer, of Strongville, OH for cover design.

Printed in the United States of America

*This Book is Dedicated
to the More Than
200 Transgender Women
Murdered
During the Year I Wrote
This Book*

 *Prologue*

I am dead. Upon my passing away some few years ago, I came here, to the afterlife, where my time has been more fully occupied than I ever would have imagined. This, I feel, is an unusual position in which to find myself, as it was always my nature to seek out any excuse for idleness (and me being officially declared "Deceased," I now have as good an excuse for idleness as anyone might desire).

Upon arrival in the afterlife, I was given a guide to help me learn what I must. My guide told me of the existence of a "Celestial Archive," containing a record of all of the people, places and events of human history. After some preliminary explanations, demonstrations and admonitions, my guide gave me permission to explore—on my own initiative— the contents of that archive. This I have done, and having spent many months searching widely throughout those records, I can tell you that I have seen much that surprised, shocked and saddened me.

In the beginning of our story, I re-visit a settlement called the Village, which is a place in the afterlife set aside only for atheists. In the Village, there are no religious or spiritual books, scriptures or observances allowed. There are no churches or other places of worship, no religious art or music, and no plays or movies which have any religious content. The unofficial leader of the Village is Satan, who (for reasons too lengthy to go into here) goes by the name "Stan."

"Then up rose Mrs. Cratchit, Cratchit's wife, dressed out but poorly in a twice-turned gown, but brave in ribbons, which are cheap and make a goodly show for sixpence ..."

CHARLES DICKENS, *A Christmas Carol*

Starting Out

I found my time spent traveling in the afterlife to be rewarding. No longer prey to those common, natural anxieties concerning my continued health and mental acuity, I came to enjoy a new sense of calm (one available only to those for whom the sting of death is but an unpleasant memory, rather than an ever-present threat). And, no longer subject to those celestial oppositions, conjunctions and retrogressions which ruled my earthly fate, I gave up at last my affiliation with the sign of Sagittarius and enjoyed a new perspective, seeing the planets from another position altogether.

Most importantly, I spent considerable time consulting the Celestial Archive. There, my natural curiosity was given over to a review of notable events and personalities of the past (revealing a fabric of complex patterns woven together out of the most commonplace materials, each embroidered with designs reflective of those fears and aspirations so

emblematic of our world). Those efforts of mine were necessarily followed by periods of repose and reflection, during which I struggled to fit so many items of rich and costly silks, brocades and leathers into my little carry-on of a soul. Nevertheless, a time did come when the memory of many warm and nurturing Christmases reasserted itself, and would not be put off. Then I went to my guide to ask his advice.

I found him reading in that place which most encourages those periodic brainstorms which nourish our imagination (that environment nevertheless providing sufficient rest, quiet and stable writing surface that such a deluge might be weathered to good purpose). That is: He was sitting at a small table in a coffee shop in (of all places!) the Village. Strolling up to him (as any more purposeful stride could not be countenanced in such a temple consecrated to conversation, contemplation and caffeine), I gained his eye, and he motioned for me to join him at the same table.

"How nice to see you," he offered, smiling. "Yes, and I am happy to see you, too," I accepted. Going on, I started right in. "Look. Here's the thing. I am having a problem. Here I am in the afterlife, where you would think my time would be consumed with 'eternal verities' and 'solutions to those unanswered mysteries of life' and even (now and then) the companionship of kings and queens and fairies. All of which is the case, I admit. But still, there is something I am missing. Something I need to revisit, so that I might recapture those feelings I used to have."

"What can be causing you so much anxiety?" he asked. "Certainly nothing has been denied to you here. So what do you find lacking?"

"Well, I miss Christmas." I explained. "I want it to be 'Christmas' the way I once knew it: That time of year which provided so much of the joy and anticipation that warmed and illuminated my childhood. But,

here, somehow everything is too 'perfect,' too 'elevated' to give me the Christmas feeling I remember."

My guide immediately jumped in, "Certainly you have not made the error of passing your time here, in the Village? You know very well the air here is too thin to permit any flame of holiday cheer to burn with any gratifying warmth."

"No, no," I agreed. "I know all too well to avoid this Village. In fact I am a bit surprised to find you here. Any reason why you choose to spend time in this particular coffee shop?" My guide smiled a sly smile (which, at the time, I attributed to some aftertaste of his coffee which, no matter how much sugar he might baptize in his cup, could never succeed in resurrecting any sweetness in the brew.)

"I will tell you my purpose later," he confided, then went on. "To be honest, I knew what was troubling you, and it seemed to me best—if we are to examine that most ancient and nurturing of holidays—that we should take up our study in the one place where we might take it out of its natural environment and study its habits and instincts in isolation. Hence, I was waiting here for you to arrive, and you being present, we can begin our task."

His thoughtfulness touched me. "Once again you anticipate my needs, and are waiting in my path to show the way. How can I thank you?" I asked. My guide (having finished his coffee) now smiled in undisguised and honest satisfaction. "Thank you for saying so," he said. "Now we should press on. Have you any thoughts on how you might approach this matter? Any prior examples you might put to use?"

I rested my chin in my palm, seeking momentary support for my weighty and burdensome confusion. At last I had an idea.

"You know," I began, "I have had good experiences consulting with some of those most well-known (even beloved) characters from literature whom I first met in life. There was that great king Ozymandias, that woodland fairy Puck, and, indeed, the Fairy Queen, herself. I don't think I could have found any better guides (present company excepted) than those expressive and (in some ways) symbolic characters from the world of arts and letters."

My guide responded, "Yes, no doubt it was that very expressiveness which the authors of those great works intended. Such eloquence as those iconic characters displayed could not be penned up in the one story of which each had so great a part. Each one having played that role assigned to him by his author, he could not afterward be prevented from galloping off to take up residence in other wide and unfenced narratives."

I continued. "Thus, it seems obvious to me that my final step in recapturing the spirit of Christmas is to find some one character—or some one story having some few, iconic personalities—who, together, sum up the inner truth and outer ceremony of Christmas."

"Yes, yes, that is an excellent plan to commence your search," my guide agreed. "Now, what story or character would you choose?"

I pondered, then replied, "There is one that immediately comes to mind. Now, I admit, any Christian believer (well-studied in Bible stories and verses) would no doubt immediately seize upon that first, identifiably 'Christmas' story. The one in which a donkey played so prominent a supporting role (bearing the weight of divinity upon his furry back). But in this exercise I feel I will more successfully reanimate that winter festival if I pick characters more nearly my contemporaries in age and culture. Thus, I could not help but select *A Christmas Carol* by Charles Dickens.

My guide was obviously both pleased and (for some reason not apparent to me) relieved to hear my choice. "Yes, it is amazing how Dickens' characters have become the center of so much of our Christmas celebration. There are those Hollywood movies re-run so many times during the season, featuring, it seems, the casting in the role of Scrooge of every able-bodied actor who is not otherwise occupied filming action-adventure 'buddy movies' or (more lucratively) infomercials. Then there are the cartoon versions for the very young, the live stage-plays (that keep those same theatres eternally solvent), and (it is painful to admit), the lunch boxes, collectibles and video games for those either too young or too easily distracted to read."

My guide went on, "But it seems to me ... if you wanted to relive the power and beauty of the story Dickens wrote, wouldn't you just ... re-read the story? Or if you were seeking to recapture some cinematic experience from your childhood which you found to be vivid and personal, wouldn't you just watch a re-run of one of those Hollywood movies which made such an impression on you? Wouldn't that be easiest, even here?"

"That's what I thought at first, and, to be honest, I have already done those things. I re-read the original story, and I did re-visit one of those movies that told the tale so well. Unfortunately, I found I had a reaction which I could not have anticipated. Where I thought I would be moved, perhaps even to tears, I found instead only impatience and exasperation. That spirit of the holidays which—when I was young—so touched me, now failed to reach me. I felt nothing—just some ill-defined annoyance at being put through those all-too-familiar scenes and revelations without any natural resolution. So ... I am frustrated, and I feel a little bit ashamed. Frustrated that I cannot find again those uplifting moments

which I know are part of the story, and ashamed that so much heartfelt love and charity fall deafly upon my hearing." Looking plaintively at my guide, I begged him, "What should I do?"

My guide sat silently, and I assumed he was contemplating how to satisfy my request. Watching his face, however, it soon became apparent to me that he was in no way formulating any solution to my problem, but instead only occupied himself looking up and down the lane on which the coffee shop was located, as if he expected the answer to march up to our table and proclaim itself. This was something I had never before seen my guide do, but I trusted him to do what was best. This being so, I also began looking up and down the lane for my savior in this time of need.

We Meet Our Host

At last, my guide and I saw who we had been waiting for, and if there is any man in all the world (this world or any other) who is less worthy of being named a "savior," I cannot think who he would be. Coming towards us up the lane, I now saw that man eternally devoted to one peculiar form of "honesty" (having promised never to tell less than half the truth), one singular form of "free choice" (always being there to offer an alternative to the godly, righteous choice), and one unconventional interpretation of the "Law" (always being there to insist upon the letter thereof, disregarding any application of its spirit). Yes, it was my old acquaintance, Stan, striding anxiously up the lane in our direction, as if the founding impulse of the Village were at stake.

Stan quickly reached us and, without observing any ceremony (there being, in the Village, all too few rituals which were so honored), he pulled a chair over to our table and sat down.

He studied me, then spoke, "So it's you, again. I haven't seen you here in quite some time." Then turning to my guide, he started in with an accusation, "You are behind this, I know. You knew that as soon as our friend here began to speak of Dickens and Scrooge and that detestable Tiny Tim, I would have no choice but to find out who was violating our rules. Well, I'm here. You got what you wanted. Now, how can I convince you—both of you—to leave and take your holiday spirits with you?"

"The truth is," my guide began (Stan and I, however, needed no such warning: my guide, we knew, was incapable of any other speech), "our friend here would benefit from hearing from you again. He has a problem

which, in any other place, I could not easily or efficiently solve, but which—here—you scramble up and serve three times before breakfast. Would you be willing to share with us some of your wisdom—and help my friend, here?"

Stan, being momentarily flattered to think that his efforts and opinions were needed (as, usually, they were little more than tolerated), he was, likewise (and to the contrary), repulsed to think that he could be expected to "help" anyone. These contrary and conflicting impulses warred within him—briefly—until (Stan being Stan) he succumbed to what he felt was nothing less than some well-earned self-congratulation ... and smiled his most willing smile.

Stan settled back in his seat, seeking a more comfortable posture from which to be begin his sermon, and (as if by some pre-arranged bit of clever stagecraft) a waiter instantly appeared at his shoulder to put a cup of coffee within his reach. Stan bent over, took a sip, and (seeming to find his coffee sufficiently bitter to suit his taste) began his speech.

"You are beginning your study of Christmas exactly where I would have counseled you," he said confidentially. "These past number of years, we have seen nothing else so universally identified with the spirit of the season that its every theme, character and identifying trope have become synonymous with the holiday. We have not failed to observe how powerful its effect has been, even on those who have never heard the story. And we cannot help but conclude that it has at last risen up into that 'heaven' of immortal, out-of-copyright 'classics' where—its faults having been so wholly forgiven it, and its virtues so glorified—that it seems destined for some eternal approbation even among that great majority of holiday revelers who have never read it."

"Wait a minute!" I interrupted. "How can anyone here have any opinion of the story or characters? It was my impression that religious works such as this were absolutely prohibited here! And I have no doubt this work would be so categorized, despite its lack of explicit Christian themes or Bible verses. How can anyone be reading *A Christmas Carol* here?"

My guide shifted uncomfortably in his seat. He was—all to obviously—worried that I would pick some sort of fight with Stan over just this sort of theological question and, like countless such disputes involving the "true meaning" of some confusingly-expressed religious prohibition, doctrine or commandment, we would end up obscuring the truth, destroying any possibility of fellowship, and taking the name of our Maker many times in vain (before finally agreeing—silently—that the other person is an idiot, and there's nothing to be done about it).

But we were lucky. Stan did not take the bait (or, thinking himself wise to the ways of the Fisherman, he went off in a wholly unexpected direction).

"Actually," he said, "where works such as this are concerned, we found long ago that we could not simply prohibit their possession in the Village. There were often too many other, non-religious purposes which such books might serve, and—frankly—their absence from our libraries here would have been far too conspicuous. Hence, after much trial and error, we found a way to keep such works as this available on-loan, while still maintaining the purity of our philosophy."

My wide-eyed puzzlement spurring him to venture on, he resumed his lesson. "Here is what I did: I selected from among all the residents here those few writers who were the most skilled in the arts of mystification,

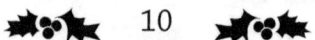

ambiguity and obfuscation. You may be sure (there being in residence many former contributors to both *The New York Review of Books* and *The New York Times* editorial page) that I had many such talented writers among whom to choose. Then, having selected three or four of the most notoriously prolix and pompous pettifoggers, I gave each of them the task of re-writing the offending book so as to make it acceptable—in content, phrasing and innuendo—for wide dissemination here. Naturally, *A Christmas Carol* was one of the first such works re-written for general consumption among our most impressionable readers."

"No doubt you are asking yourself," Stan helpfully observed, "how it could be that *A Christmas Carol*—which takes as its theme the vitality and restorative power of that holiday—might be re-written to remove those very qualities. How, indeed, could any story—retaining such memorable and (to some) appealing characters as Bob Cratchit and that detestable Tiny Tim—be so remade that those characters (being placed in jeopardy) the reader might remain indifferent to their fate?"

"Now, in the beginning, we did have some difficulty in finding a formula for revising this classic work. Then, Dickens being Dickens, we found a way. It is often remarked—and I do not voice any criticism of the author by saying so—that Dickens was wonderfully adept at creating vivid, humorous and unforgettable 'caricatures.' By which I mean, he did not so much seek to portray complex, living souls as he did rather strive to imagine more-or-less representative and sui generis 'types.' Writing at the time he did and for the readership he had, he employed all of his humor and wit to create—in admirably few words—characters who might serve the purpose for which he (the author) created them."

"Thus, we soon saw that, starting with such 'caricatures' (their characteristic features being all too subject to alteration), we could, first, readily change this or that aspect of one of the story's important characters. Then, going on to make appropriate, corresponding alterations to those other characters with whom that person interacted, we were able to wholly change the drift and moral of the story. So, in short," he summarized, "we do have a version of *A Christmas Carol* here, but it is one you would hardly recognize."

Stan paused to take a sip of his coffee, and, appearing to find it tasteless, cold and bitter, he was thereby energized to continue his account. He smiled his slyest smile, then ventured, "Now, if you will indulge me," (which … he being well-acquainted with the faults and weaknesses of ordinary men and women, he was all too certain would be done), "I will relate that story."

My guide and I having been rendered speechless in awe (and, it must be said, paralyzed with dread), Stan prepared to summarize that counterfeit version of *A Christmas Carol* which he passed off as genuine upon unsuspecting readers in the Village.

"Now, I will not be able to re-tell the story in its entirety," Stan commenced. "We do not have the time, and I do not claim to remember its every rich and memorable detail. So what I will do is this. I will ask you … " he said, turning in my direction, "to briefly summarize—one-by-one—some few of the most unique and representative scenes, including (we must not omit) those most significant turning-points which give the story its power. Then, after you have given your best and most life-like summary of each such scene, I will tell you how we handle that scene in our re-written version."

I Begin the Story

At last I was ready to speak. "You know, Stan, whatever other reservations I may have concerning the rules you have here in the Village, I have to admit to nothing less than admiration for the thorough and consistent manner in which you enforce those rules. Thus I am certain the re-written version of *A Christmas Carol* must be very much altered from the one so often re-visited by Hollywood. I assume that, although you will have modified the characters, the conflict, the resolution and (it goes without saying) the 'moral,' you will not have altogether changed the structure of the story."

"This structure we all know well. We first meet Scrooge on the day before Christmas, and we see him involved in several characteristically miserly, tightfisted and skinflint behaviors which, seeing them in any friend or close acquaintance, we put upon our face our most accusatory scowl and call that person 'Scrooge.' We see him suffer the visitation of that foreshadowing spirit who used to be his partner. Then being unable to avoid sleep (which, he feared, would but open the door to those promised supernatural materializations), we see him drift off at last."

"After this, the story gives us a most instructive flashback, where the Ghost of Christmas Past takes Scrooge (and us) back to the time when Scrooge was just starting out in school. Then more events are given—gradually taking us along with Scrooge as he gets older and more established in life—until at last we meet the second spirit (Ghost of Christmas Present Day). Going on, the story takes us into the future, to some Christmas when we see that Scrooge, himself, has passed away. Once the author is done moving us backward and forward in time—visiting years long ago and others yet to be—he resumes his story. We re-join Scrooge on Christmas morning (Present Day) and we see his changed nature and resurrected heart. So this story is not uncomplicated, especially as to date and place and season, and makes demand upon the reader that he does not lose his place."

"Stan, I am supposing that—however much you have re-written this odyssey—you are faithful enough to the story (however unfaithful you are to every other truth) that you, too, will take the reader back to see Scrooge at that time when he was a young student. And you, too, will have Scrooge visit those same locations, meeting or bringing along the same characters, and (as you have explained) changing only so much of the story that the 'moral' intended by the author might be wholly spoiled, obscured and contradicted."

I paused to give Stan the opportunity to set me right, if I had seriously gone off the tracks, but he only smiled a wry smile as if to say, "It's your funeral."

Boarding School

"**V**ery well then," I agreed. "The first two scenes which are pivotal to the story are these: In the beginning, we find Scrooge as a young boy, left all alone at Christmastime in the study hall at his boarding school. We see him brooding mournfully, feeling abandoned by his friends (who have already left to be with their families for the holidays). We are shown how much Scrooge suffered from this privation. So much so that—in his boyish imagination—he took refuge in some of the stories he had

read in class involving princes, pirates and brave adventurers from for-
eign lands."

"Then the next scene shown to us is in some ways similar. We see
Scrooge now considerably older, but still a prisoner in some rank, unpleasant and unsanitary boarding school which (like the first) strove to
make of Scrooge a perfect example of a 'well-rounded gentleman' (being
humorless, grim and pedantic not only in English but in Latin and Greek,
as well). In this case, however, we see that Scrooge's younger sister,
Fanny, has been sent with a coach to bring Scrooge home from this place
of exile. Scrooge is genuinely and unreservedly grateful to see Fanny, and
he acknowledges how much he owes her for interceding on his behalf
with their father."

"Summing up, we see that Scrooge was not brought up a miser, nor
was he born lacking his appointed share of human warmth or emotion.
We see him suffer from that very isolation and abandonment which (in
later years) he sought out for himself. We see him as a child happy and
grateful to have been loved and cared for by his sister. How (we ask) can
his heart have come to be devoid of all those warm and gentle mercies
which she once bestowed upon him?"

"Thus, we are shown that Scrooge was a miser 'made' not 'born.' Seeing him (a child) suffering loneliness and want, and likewise witnessing
his tender feelings for his sister, we are warned that some great revolu-
tion is to be expected in Scrooge's heart. Such feelings as he once had,
having in them the power of growth and regeneration, we know may not
easily be uprooted, no matter how cold and grasping the hand that seeks
to strip those branches."

A Young Man

"The next two scenes in the story—shown to Scrooge and to us by the Ghost of Christmas Past—are active, joyous and full of life. The Ghost takes Scrooge to the place of business of Scrooge's first employer, Mr. Fezziwig. We see Scrooge a vital young man having a good friend and fellow apprentice with whom he could share his struggles and ambitions. We are permitted to attend a wonderful Christmas Eve dance organized and presided over by that benevolent, fun-loving couple, Mr. and Mrs. Fezziwig. The author spares no detail describing the dance, and suggesting thereby that this first tentative discovery by Scrooge of the opposite sex was an experience not lost upon his developing passions. The author underlines this truth: Scrooge was no bloodless, calculating cipher, but a young man on the threshold of manhood."

"The next scene picks up (as if) seamlessly from the first. We are shown Scrooge meeting with a comely young woman—Belle—near his age and (it is suggested) well-matched to Scrooge in prospect and temperament. From the content of their conversation on this occasion (of which I will say more in a moment), we quickly grasp that Scrooge and Belle have made a sort of 'commitment to be committed.' Not a full engagement, but a kind of promise to (some day) fly up to that 'perch' (in life) from which a man and woman might commence that great migration which begins a romantic 'union of two lovebirds' and finishes up a chaotic gaggle of squawking, flocking, flapping little peeps."

"Now, necessarily, we conclude that—at some recent, earlier time— Scrooge found within his heart amorous feelings for Belle, and that he pursued her until she—being convinced that he possessed those stead-fast, trustworthy qualities only to be looked for in eligible bachelors—gently guided him to that novel idea (foremost in Belle's most precious dreams since childhood) that two people feeling as they did about each other are destined to be 'one.'"

That Fateful Error

"**W**e have not, as you are aware, finished with that scene wherein we see Scrooge and Belle parted. This scene introduces us to 'Scrooge'—the heartless, avaricious miser. We meet that Scrooge who has put away all thoughts of warm and loving human relationships, and who has raised up a Golden Idol in their place. We see Belle confront Scrooge, bravely naming that error to which Scrooge has already (out of scene) bound himself in arid and unproductive devotion. Scrooge, far from denying this profoundest change in the man (himself) she knew and to whom she promised all, baldly confesses his obedience to that new god who rules his life."

"The author does not show us the time or place or occasion of this great and fateful error by Scrooge, but only gives his readers these two scenes—the dance at Fezziwig's, before, and the parting from Belle, after—which they might see as gateposts demarking his entry into that dark, descending destiny prefiguring death. We are not shown how Scrooge could have come to such a painful, self-defeating fault (that chooses loneliness in place of love). We only know that he did."

Stan Begins His Story

Having come this far, I felt it was time to hear from Stan how those scenes which I had already described might be handled in Stan's version of *A Christmas Carol*. "Perhaps you should jump in now," I said to Stan. "I don't want to go so far ahead that we forget where we've been."

"Yes, fine," Stan granted. "Although, in this case, I actually have very little to add—or should I say 'change'—about these first few scenes involving Scrooge's childhood. Of the first scene—in the boarding school—my only change is to emphasize how greatly this early experience shaped Scrooge's character—extending its influence even into his old age. Being left alone and having no other outlet than to study and improve his mind demonstrated to Scrooge that the path to his future could best be found through learning, knowledge and achievement. Putting Scrooge to the side for the moment, how many other biographies of 'great men' have we read that show a time of childhood want and privation, after which the young man in question soon embarks upon some life-long career involving some great achievements in science, commerce or government? So, indeed, we see there was nothing out of the ordinary in Scrooge's reaction to the boarding school."

"Now, this same approach I have continued over into the second 'boarding school' scene, where Fanny comes to bring Scrooge home. Here, however, I would emphasize how timely is this visit by Fanny, it being made clear that by this point, Scrooge has learned all that this crude and rural boarding school has to teach. And of Scrooge's gratitude for Fanny's efforts to free him from this prison—why, I would not change a thing! Certainly Fanny—who, as a young woman of the time would never have been granted any opportunity to learn or study or improve her mind—could not help but sacrifice her own (undeveloped) talents in service of this man (her brother) who, by all his hard work in school, has made himself her 'better' in this and many other ways."

No Error Here

"**N**ow we come to the greatest change of all," Stan portentously announced. "This is the most profound alteration in the story which, without this change, we could not admit this holiday drama into that pantheon of tautological truth we worship in our Village. This is the change: You have rightly pointed out that, in Dickens' version, there is (off stage) some fundamental 'choice' which Scrooge has made which he (the author) makes us comprehend without our having seen or heard or read it. How else could Dickens, at the end of the story, propose that Scrooge could undergo his soul's entire redemption, a change so complete and profound that the reader cannot help but be charmed by the effect?"

"But in our story, there is no 'choice' that we infer! Scrooge makes no 'fateful error.' Indeed, no error here at all! What has he done but seize those implements by which he might rake in the world's increase to his own private storehouse of prosperity? Why shouldn't he—having labored in that shabby boarding school—put the fruits of those labors solely in his own pocket? Why, what other aspiration could he have? This ... orphan child of his no doubt uneducated, poor and unaccomplished mother, whom we are given to understand stole selfishly off in childbirth to lie within some unremembered, unremarked and unacknowledged grave?

Should he not try to better himself!? Should he, having all these inborn talents handed down to him as his birthright, have any other ambition than to turn them to his sole account?"

"In the story which we turn to here, we see no choice … no error … no fault. We find only those customary, appropriate and (in all ways) rightful inherited male advantages, which—as our readers here affirm—Scrooge would be a fool to share."

Belle Is Dismissed

"This next scene," Stan allows, "begins the place where we have made multiple changes—not only in emphasis but also in outcome and motivation. When Scrooge parts from Belle, we no longer place the blame upon Scrooge who, in these circumstances, has done nothing more or less than what any ambitious man in his position would do."

"In our new version, we see Belle trying to entangle Scrooge in her (seductive) scheme; seeking to tempt Scrooge into that conjugal indenture by which he would be expected to place his private fortune at risk of her negotiable bill and note. She, having no remunerative prospects to match against his, why would he see a partnership with her as one promising his pecuniary enrichment? Like Fanny, we expect that Belle has only the most meagre education. So, really, where is the common ground upon which they might conceive any fruitful domestic intercourse? What can she offer him but financial burdens dolled up by her as bundles of joy? Where is the profit in that?"

Stan warms to his argument, "No! It is Scrooge who rejects her! It is Scrooge who presses that advantage (seized and exploited by every other member of his sex) to use his every hereditary privilege to his personal and particular gain. Scrooge will not fall victim to that original error (chargeable not only against Belle but against every other member of her benevolent sorority) by which—offering to him (in private) some ripe and fertile fruit—she would but pick his pocket."

My guide and I sat perfectly still. Looking down in the direction of the ground, our heads were bowed in painful self-awareness; we having been involuntary witness to this latest, inescapable evidence (despite of which, we know Stan scorns to stipulate) of those unjust and unrecorded burdens which our gender's self-importance has placed upon Eve's fair and guileless progeny. However, there being seated at our table no representative of that divinely-appointed gender to whom we might abase ourselves in humble expiation, we only waited, each of us silently reliving some instance in which we had disappointed our mothers.

Our Cups Refilled

The effect of my hearing the substance of Stan's most-recently-explained improvements to Dickens' *Christmas Carol* was profound. He had, to my mind, come so near to his presumed intent of exorcising the Christmas spirit from the tale that I despaired of its ever being heard again. And yet, I had to marvel that Stan—beginning with an uplifting story of regret, renewal and redemption—could make of that silk purse a sow's ear of avarice, arrogance and unapologetic financial solipsism. I could not help but pause a few moments, trying to recover my poise enough so that I might pick up the story at that place where I had left it (before Stan pulled off its wings to see if he could make it fly).

My guide sensed my reluctance—if not outright inability—to begin again. He called to have our cups refilled (a play for time) then ... he made small talk with Stan: "You know, Stan, I must compliment you on the coffee you serve here. No matter what flavor or variety or place-of-origin the beans, it always has the taste of last week's grounds." Our cups refilled—and Stan having nodded in grateful appreciation of this rare compliment launched in his direction by my guide—I found my guide's concern for me had so percolated through to my heart that I was stimulated to go on.

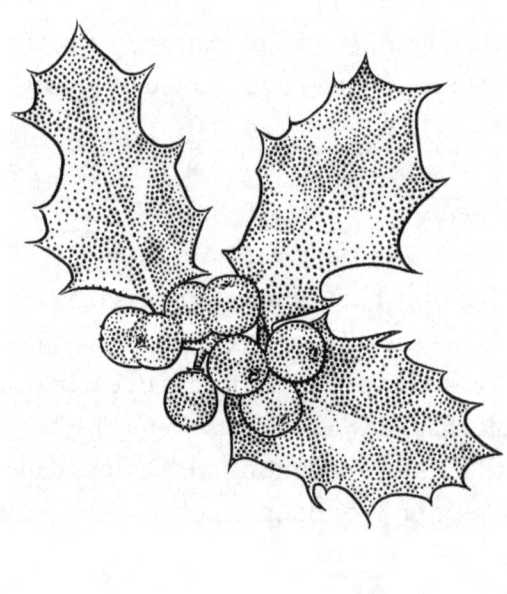

That Bless'd Feast

Thus I resumed. "The next section which is most integral to the sum and total of the story is, of course, the Christmas feast at the home of Bob Cratchit. We are introduced to all the members of his little family, and we see revealed those bonds of love and care that bind them all together. We meet, first, Mrs. Cratchit, who is feverishly busy with the preparations necessary to bring the goose and pudding to perfection. We see her helped in many ways by her eldest daughter, Martha (recently released from her daily labor as an apprentice in a dress shop)."

"We meet the second daughter, Belinda, who we see manage domestic chores we would have thought beyond her years. There are as well, we are shown, two younger children (boy and girl) whose names we are not given, but whose energy, enthusiasm and diligence cannot be doubted despite their youth. Remembering that London is a city in a realm where primogeniture is more than just a word we hope to use while playing Scrabble, we are then introduced to the eldest male Cratchit, named Peter (hereditary steward of the Cratchit estates: being four rooms occupied at leasehold, determinable as of the end of any month upon deficiency of rent, no life estate reserved, no lives by any charity preserved)."

Now, at this point in my summary of this immortal Christmas parable, I came to that point in the story which I could sense would most upset our host. Our previous conversation, reflecting as it did the first use I had ever heard of the word "detestable" as both an honorific and an epithet, I was loath to press on and introduce the next character—without first smoothing the way with Stan.

Turning to him, I proffered this transparent and apologetic plea: "You know, Stan, there is one more member of the Cratchit family I have not addressed, but he being so well known, I wonder if I need to bother … ?" Then Stan surprised me. "No, no, go right ahead," he instantly shot back. "There is no reason not to tell the whole story, and that requires you to tell even about that little … limp and simpering gimp."

I sat dumfounded. Here was Stan, whose character, we knew, was so imbued with his own unique idea of "fairness" that, some other person's very life depending upon what Stan has on offer, he would not hear of accepting any other payment than the full, undiscounted, fair market value thereof (there being, in Stan's world, no word for "charity"). I saw in this case (as I had seen in so many others), that he could not set my mind at ease (spreading his own suffocating version of "calm" across the surface of my disordered thoughts), unless he were permitted to prescribe for me a "cure" which (tasting it) did burn my lips and sting my tongue.

"Very well then," I said. "The final member of the Cratchit household we have to meet is Tiny Tim, who is introduced to the reader on the shoulders of his father, Bob Cratchit. Now, Tiny Tim's youth, weakness and disability being foremost among those attributes which the author wishes us to see and remember, we cannot be misled into finding (in him) any other model than that other tiny, innocent creature who was likewise carried into some poor and humble dwelling upon a back bent low by constant labor."

"We see that Tiny Tim was by far the youngest and the least capable of assisting in the cooking and serving of the feast. What is more, his very presence delays the work, as the two youngest children are required to leave off helping their mother in order to take him out to the kitchen

in back to watch the pudding bubble. But, despite his being the least able to bear up his share of the cooking, carrying, carving, consuming, clearing and cleaning, there is no doubt who (in the author's intention) bears up the greatest burden of restoring Scrooge's soul."

Taking out a small pocket reprint of the story, I turned to the familiar page and read those immortal words spoken of Tiny Tim by his father:

"He told me, coming home, that he hoped the people saw him in the church, because he was a cripple, and it might be pleasant to them to remember upon Christmas Day, who made lame beggars walk, and blind men see."

Silently, I asked myself how it could happen that such a large and generous soul might be propped-up upon no more than one ill-fitting iron leg brace and one wobbly little crutch.

Now speaking aloud, I continued, "The portrayal by Dickens of the feast is so skillfully measured out and seasoned by the author that the reader is treated to multiple, contrasting flavors coming together in one savory dish. We see how inadequate is the quantity of food (despite its skillful preparation by Mrs. Cratchit). The goose we are told is on the scrawny side, the pudding altogether too small, and the wassail watered down and weak. Nevertheless, we see how the family's good spirits, their love for each other, and their devotion to the Christmas holiday, overcome every other inadequacy and make this day a feast in celebration of gratitude for their Savior. This scene showing the Cratchit family at feasting sets the bar for every later author, film director and playwright who might wish to portray a scene of family and domestic bliss. There is none other like it."

Stan Explains

Thus was my abbreviated description of the Cratchit's Christmas feast brought to a close without interruption. All the while I was talking, however, my guide and I could not help noticing how more and more uncomfortable Stan was becoming. We knew this was, first, due to his urgency to finish up his interview with me and speed me on to my way to my next destination outside the Village. But, more importantly, it shortly became clear to me that Stan—having had to sit quietly and listen to my brief but vivid outline of the Christmas tale—could not avoid being reminded of many unpleasant memories involving: cozy fires with stocking hung in front, glowing decorated trees surrounded by jumbles of bright and sparkling packages, and (the worst) those hymns which cheerful voices shared exalting "peace on earth, good will toward men." But, my efforts to bring to life the Cratchits and their feast being completed, it was now Stan's turn to play storyteller.

"Yes, well," he said (tiptoeing up to the point he wished to make), "that was … adequate … and only what I should have expected." His tone was such that he might, instead, have been warning us, "Well … if you let your dog eat tinsel, don't be surprised if you need a new rug."

"But let me plunge on in," Stan resumed. "We have come to that place in our story—and by that I mean the version of *A Christmas Carol* which we have here in the Village—where we necessarily take leave of many familiar aspects of the original story and strike out on our own. There are multiple reasons for this, of which I will tell you only those which suit my purpose."

"First, and most obviously, the original story was published in 1843, and our present age is far removed from that year. It is my goal to fill our libraries here with books that will appeal to our residents, and, frankly, however much you 'outsiders' may love the story, even you must admit it includes many words and terms and references which are poorly understood by people of today. You mean to retain the old story in its worn and threadbare costume, while we, on the other hand, not being inhibited in any way, have no hesitation in tarting it up in the latest provocative and revealing fashions (as, here, we do not say 'slut' as if it were a bad thing)."

"Our next compelling reason for making wholesale changes in the story is, simply, that any other approach would violate that unwritten and unspoken understanding (which even we do not dare to contravene) that the scenes, dialogue and characters of any story must be matched to the time and place and era in which the action is placed. That is, we cannot transport a pre-Industrial Age businessman and moneylender (educated in Physic, Latin, Rhetoric and Greek) to 21st Century London. We cannot uproot a poor, 19th Century extended family and plop them down lost, confused and disoriented into our Virtual, Digital Age. Thus, having brought Scrooge up-to-date with 21st Century misogyny, we cannot avoid bringing all the other trappings of this story up-to-date, as well."

"Here is the final and, I believe, most compelling reason I have brought this fable up to present-day. And, it is a reason which I claim (with some modest pride) to be one unique to us here in the Village." [Stan, having—in his mind—spoken those words as if he whispered some prophetic truth, in fact, his face and posture swelled and boomed with self-important boasting, reminding my guide and me of some (other) horned (and rutting) ungulate proclaiming his domain.]

"Put in barest terms," he went on, "the moral of this story, the underlying conflict, and the supposed transformation which Scrooge undergoes, all these things are no more than anachronisms in our world. It is not so much that we, here in the Village, reject and disbelieve the Christmas message (although, you may be sure, we do). It is, rather, that we do not any longer find it probable … or plausible or even … feasible that any real person (such as Scrooge) would ever say or think or choose those things the author makes him do. That long-ago 'Christmastime' (featuring all the time-worn customs, rituals and devotions of that Bible-reading age) would be unrecognizable to those brought up in our multi-cultural, multi-racial and (unofficially) agnostic world."

The Cratchit Contemporary Feast

"The feast begins!" proclaimed Stan. "Just as we know that every feast-day must begin with some locally anticipated sunrise, so must every feast begin with its first celebrant—who, in this case, as in its model, is Mrs. Cratchit. We see her lying back in her lounger in her modest living room, a can of soda within easy reach of her left hand, and her cell phone resting convenient to her right. Despite my starting off this scene with talk of sunrise, in fact the time of day is nearly sundown. Nevertheless, the room is well-lit by the ever-present glow from the TV set, whose volume has been muted so as not to intrude upon Mrs. Cratchit's nap."

"The house—modest though it may be—is nearly silent (if we do not count the rhythmic wheeze of Mrs. Cratchit's breathing, evidence of her youthful years when she was a smoker—her habit now temporarily quieted by that satisfying patch which she wears over her skull-and-crossbones tattoo). But you would be mistaken if you thought her alone in the room. No. In fact, looking more closely about the living room, we see two small bodies cuddled up asleep on the couch amidst multiple, colorful (empty) candy wrappers (all of them the same color as those spots of drool pooling beneath each child's lips). Is this not a scene of quiet, restful domestic bliss?" Stan asked, rhetorically.

"But it would be a poor feast, indeed (even here in our Village, where no natural human appetite is ever properly satisfied), if this were the whole of it. No. The back door opens (we do not see; it is in the kitchen, on the other side of the cabinets next to the TV in that room) and in comes Martha, eldest daughter of the Cratchit family. She is breathless from running, but we see her take great pains to quickly locate the two small children earlier introduced (who, in Dickens' tale, are not named; but here, to forestall confusion, we will give their names—being Jason and Ja'nelle). Seeing the children sleeping, Martha at once takes ever greater care to keep silent and not wake them. She glides through the kitchen and down the hallway to what we suppose must be her bedroom. Then in a remarkably short time (considering the total transformation of Martha's appearance), she re-emerges from her bedroom, slips silently back down the hall, passes (un-noticed) through the kitchen, and slips noiselessly out the back door."

"Now, her appearance, which I expect you will want to know, is easily described. Coming in, she is appareled in a skin-tight, elastic tube-top, in a color usually to be seen in life preservers, traffic cones and prison smocks. Below her waist, she wears a skirt—the hem of which (offering welcome and convenience to her boldest admirers) comes closer to her elbows than her knees. Finally, her figure is liberally decorated with silvery, glittery costume jewelry consisting of necklaces, bracelets, earrings and (apparently randomly located) piercings. Her outfit thus informs the world she is employed at a small franchise shop in the local mall, where she specializes in piercing the ears of young girls proven to be old enough to have purchased a fake ID. But, Martha, going out, was on her own time, and (no longer bound to those dull and drab sartorial requirements of her employer), she now took the opportunity to change into a shorter skirt, a tighter top, freshly teased-up hair, and eye make-up that would have been considered excessive by a performer in a drag show (giving to her face all the exotic and mysterious sensuality of a sleep-deprived raccoon)."

Stan leaned back in his chair, took a sip of coffee, and (narrowing his eyes) confronted my guide and me over those accusatory thoughts he believed we entertained. "You seem to be thinking that Martha, in this case, was somehow overcome with love and consideration for her younger brother and sister, and that she kept as silent as she did out of tender feelings for her siblings. Nothing could be further from the truth. In fact, Jason and Ja'nelle are not her siblings at all—they are her own natural children, whom she brought into this world while still a student in the local school. And, it is the case of each such child that Martha (no doubt distracted at the crucial moments), left the names and identities of their fathers back in school with all the other names and dates and kings and queens and wars and treaties which made so little impression upon her."

"Now, lest you think that Mrs. Cratchit will be permitted to sleep right through the feast, I call your attention, again, to the back (kitchen) door through which now comes Belinda, second eldest of the Cratchit daughters, accompanied by her friend, Karey. Do not, however, imagine that Mr. and Mrs. Cratchit allow their younger daughter to dress in the same loose and casual clothing (matching her developing morals; being, again, 'loose and casual') as her elder sister Martha. No. We see that Belinda wears those items of apparel—indeed, a uniform—in a style and colors required of all female students at the middle school which she attends."

"Below her waist, she wears a skirt which dips demurely to no more than two inches above her knee (or, honestly, would have, had she not rolled the waistband up three times). Her blouse, as well (white, short sleeves, buttons up the front), was likewise demure (or, honestly, would have been two years ago, when it nearly fit), though now—her developing chest having added several inches to her womanly allure—the day-to-day status of those buttons ('Have you seen them today? Are they still there?'), had become a wondrous, mystifying, unexplainable point-of-fascination amongst Belinda's male classmates."

"Belinda strode smartly up to her mother's lounger and commenced kicking it—hard enough, she hoped, to wake her mother up without alerting the two sleeping children. In due course, Mrs Cratchit was roused from her nap by Belinda's increasingly vigorous kicks involving, in the end, some poking of her patch. Belinda, being in this case sensitive to her mother's need for sleep, only whispered 'I need money. Right now. I'm going out.' Then, she gave a sort of nod in the direction of Karey, so that her mother would know she needed to hurry, as there was someone waiting. (In fact, since coming into the Cratchit household, Karey had not ceased having her nose buried in her smart-phone screen, where texts and photos—and necessary replies—occupied her full attention until that time—but moments hence—when she and Belinda took leave of the Cratchit feast.)"

"Mrs. Cratchit did at last come back to consciousness and, seeing her daughter in some advanced state of agitation bordering on hysteria, at once intuited that her daughter wanted money to go to the mall. Mrs. Cratchit (cognizant of the two sleeping children) mimed-out for her daughter that familiar, domestic drama wherein she found her purse, took out her wallet, opened it, and took out some money. Belinda, ever the attentive student of modern, amateur theatre, at once hurried over to where her mother always kept her purse. There she acted out for her audience (Karey) that drama which her mother had only just rehearsed.

After which performance, the whole assembly (both Belinda and Karey) feeling enriched in many ways by that amateur theatrical performance, promptly left by the back door."

Stan, we could see, was becoming a bit fatigued. He had been speaking for some little while, and his coffee cup was now empty. My guide seeing this, he considerately motioned for one of the waitresses to come over and refill his cup. This she did, walking up to the table with a coffee carafe in each hand (the one in her left hand having that characteristic orange plastic handle and lid). She smiled at Stan and asked, "Would you like 'Regular Dirt' (proffering the carafe with the black handle) or 'Dishwater' (proffering the orange)?" Stan—seeming to need that extra jolt of muddy swill—selected the "Regular." Then he went on.

"I can foresee," he said, looking from my guide to me and back again, "that you are only waiting for the opportune moment to complain that, having promised to show you the Cratchit family Christmas Feast, I have shortchanged you one, important adult Cratchit. That is, you are no doubt anxiously studying the kitchen door, expecting at any moment to see Bob Cratchit make his entrance. But, in my story, you must not expect to be rewarded in accordance with your efforts, nor yet (trusting you will be forgiven your debts in the same measure wherewith you forgive others) will you receive that judgment to which you believe yourself entitled. This is my story, and I am telling it."

"In my story," Stan provocatively proclaimed, "it is time to meet another Cratchit (one who, to my mind, is always and everywhere as 'detestable' as such innocent, modest creatures invariably are). So, next," he started up again, "the back door once more opens and two young boys enter. They tiptoe in, as if they expect to find the residents at home, but

napping (as they did). The boy nearest the living room spies Mrs. Cratchit and, seeing her notice him as well, gives a small and tentative wave in her direction. She instantly (and responsively) points in the direction of the cabinet over in the corner of the kitchen."

"The first boy, seeming to be guided by some oft-repeated tradition which he (a visitor) knows to be observed in the Cratchit household—opens the cabinet and, taking out the bread and a jar of peanut butter, commences to make three sandwiches. These being assembled, he forthwith wraps them up in paper towels. Meanwhile, his companion finds three unspoken-for bananas, three cans of soda, and one unopened package of cookies. Gathering these rare and costly treasures, this caravan of visitors-from-afar trudges off in the direction of one of the back bedrooms (the TV screen being the only guiding star by which they find their way)."

"The boys soon find the bedroom which they know well. At home is that youngest Cratchit, Tiny Tim. There they find him, comfortable in his wheelchair, sitting directly in front of a big-screen TV monitor and holding in his hands a game controller by which, at that very moment, he has ascended to yet a higher level of the game, having slain dozens of hideous alien adversaries to reach that place. Such an achievement, he knows (when his friends learn of it), they will (once more) commence shouting, clamoring and praising those names he uses in the game, being 'Tiny Tim, Destroyer of Worlds!' and 'Tiny Tim, The Annihilator!' and (his favorite) 'Tiny Tim, Bringer of Death!'"

"Back in the living room, the cell phone within Mrs. Cratchit's reach briefly comes alive, playing some bright snippet of that holiday classic in which the singer laments the news that, 'Santa got run over by a beer truck.' Mrs. Cratchit grabs the phone and—seeing her husband's name on the screen—cheerfully answers 'What do you want?'"

Stan went on, "Since we cannot, by any rights, eavesdrop upon the other side of this conversation, I will merely summarize it by saying that Bob Cratchit has called to let his wife know that—this being Christmas Day, and the big-box discount store at which Bob works being scheduled to be open 24 hours over Christmas—he, Bob, will have to stay at work until the end of his shift the next morning. Thus, he apologizes, he will be unable to pick up the pizza which they had earlier agreed to share as their Christmas feast."

"Mrs. Cratchit expressed disappointment: first, that she had been looking forward to that pizza; second, that she would thereby have to watch Jason and Ja'nelle all by herself; and, third, that Bob would not be home when (as she expected) Peter stopped by the house later. Oh, one more thing, she thought (after she hung up with him): She would miss him."

"Just moments after hanging up with Bob, Mrs. Cratchit's phone rings again. She sees the caller's name on the screen and blurts out, 'Speak of the Devil!'" (Stan—all too evidently—was especially proud of this little touch of irony.)

Stan went on, "She answered, 'Peter, where are you? When are you coming?' Then, her face reflected disappointment, as she heard that Peter would not be able to get away, and he would have to pick up the presents sometime tomorrow. He said he had to go, then hung up."

"This was, this day, Mrs. Cratchit's greatest disappointment. Putting the phone down, she looked over to the corner of the room where, once, years before, they had had a proper Christmas tree (but not for a long time, now). In that corner she could see still resting where she had put them down (fresh from the outlet store, and still boasting that brand-name upon all the wrapping) some four or five goodly-sized boxes containing trucks and guns and plastic dinosaurs."

"These packages she had purchased for Peter, so that, when he went over to the home of the parents of that young woman who was the mother of his child (though 'not yet'—and maybe 'never'—'wife'), he would not arrive empty-handed at their Christmas celebration, but would have gifts to give his son. But now, she thought, he'll have to do that tomorrow, if he has time (which usually he does not … for domestic obligations such as this). As a result of this discouraging news, Mrs. Cratchit was stung with a sense of bitter disappointment, as if, having nurtured in her imagination a picture of herself dazzled and delighted to be the center of attention at some elaborate surprise party given in her honor, she was instead asked to pick up the check."

"Turning her head in the direction of the TV (the sole illumination in the room), she found the remote and once-more hit the 'Mute' button. There was, on the screen, some tenth re-run of the most-recent version of Dickens' *A Christmas Carol*, and at that very instant, on-screen, was Tiny Tim. That detestable after-dinner speaker now being given his cue, Mrs. Cratchit heard him say:"

'God Bless us every one!'

"These words were all that Jason and Ja'nelle needed to bring them back to wakefulness, and they at once clamored to be fed. Mrs. Cratchit, being an attentive mother and a more-than-adequate babysitter,

promptly set about feeding them that dinner which they had not expected but which, thereafter when they spoke of it, brought back to them all the wonder and contentment of the Christmas season.

Mrs. Cratchit poured out two bowls of dry, sugary breakfast cereal. Then looking in the refrigerator for milk, she found in its place only a half-empty carton of eggnog. At first frustrated, but then deciding that Tiny Tim had it right after all, she poured the remainder of the eggnog on the cereal—and served it to them, just like that."

The Critics Opine

Stan finished speaking and, by the silence which ensued, it gradually became clear to me that he was expecting either to be begged "Please go on," or (more likely), to be congratulated upon a "tale well-told." However, it soon became evident that Stan's usual uncanny ability to size-up his listener (who, in this case, was me) and to offer just that one inducement which might bring forth the response he wanted, failed him. Howsoever Stan might have wished me to respond, he could not have anticipated (or desired) what I actually said.

"Yikes!" I expostulated. "I never expected that! When you said you were going to introduce a few changes to Dickens' well-known caricatures—and thereby change the moral of the story—you were (in this sole instance, I am sure) telling the whole (not just the preponderance) of the truth." I sat momentarily dazed, as if, having just finished consuming a hearty Christmas feast of turkey, dressing and pumpkin pie, the cook revealed to me it was but flavored, textured tofu.

At last I felt I was "myself" enough to resume our earlier discussion. "To begin with, I don't see how we can continue our agreed arrangement of me summarizing some well-loved or critical-to-the-story scenes in the original, and then you contrasting that exposition with your own account of the corresponding scenes in your version."

"I mean … what is the point of my talking about those scenes which reflect Scrooge's callous disregard for the poor … or those scenes which depend upon Scrooge witnessing the fruits of his lonely, miserly life? We already know there is no 'vacant seat in the chimney-corner' nor any 'crutch without an owner' to be found in the Cratchit dwelling. So that whole scene just fails for want of motivation."

"We might imagine that Ghost of Christmas Yet to Come taking Scrooge to visit his tombstone, but I do not believe he (or we) would derive the same message if we knew that Scrooge (in life) had spent his fortune freely (he never having been a 'miser'). Indeed, we know that any man of our modern day who is possessed of any considerable fortune (being first, we know, in want of an ex-wife) is likewise expected to practice philanthropy—to endow a 'chair' at a university or a new wing of a hospital, or some other such capital investment in his public reputation."

"Now, what the original story would tell us is the primary beneficiary of Scrooge's new-found charitable spirit (or, I should say, 'who') is, of course, Tiny Tim. In the story, it is only Scrooge's generosity which saves Tiny Tim from an early grave. But, Stan, I have already guessed what will be the outcome in your story, and it is an outcome which any of us might see pre-figured in Dickens' classic version. We cannot forget those few, brief words which epitomize Scrooge's selfish, self-justifying evasion of his Christian duty. He says:

'Are there no prisons? Are there no workhouses?'"

"But in your new, contemporary and socially-responsible version, we hear him say, instead:

'Are there no social service agencies? Are there no charity hospitals?'"

"These words Scrooge might say in all innocence. Yes, there are today social-service agencies which are (reasonably) well-funded, and which have as one of their missions to provide services to those (like Tiny Tim) who are disabled or infirm. And there are charitable hospitals, as well, which regularly perform just that very surgery which might allow Tiny Tim to walk again."

"It is unarguable, Stan, that by bringing the *Christmas Carol* story up to present-day, you have, perhaps without intending it (although I have my doubts), altogether spoiled the whole thing."

That Painful Truth

I had come to a place where escape seemed impossible. Then, Stan being Stan, he helpfully pointed out that, not only was escape not possible, but being where I was, ruin was inevitable.

"I know very well what you two were attempting here," he challenged us. "I know that, in some misguided effort to re-capture the Christmas Spirit, you thought to come here (where it is not otherwise to be found) and, by speaking of it, and thinking about it, and chewing it over to its own extremity, you might discover how it works, where it failed, and how you might recover it. But you are much deluded if you think that any such emotional dramatization of the Christmas Spirit could long exist in this Village without me having my way with it. I have no patience with such things! You can no more isolate *A Christmas Carol* in this Village than you can a box of jelly donuts in a police station."

"Nevertheless," Stan charitably allowed (something I had never before seen him do), "I do understand your perplexity, and in an effort to show my 'good faith'..." [My guide and I were momentarily stunned when ... at that very instant, Stan's features were utterly transformed! He seemed to have been possessed by some powerful, involuntary seizure, causing his left eye to twitch uncontrollably and his head to jerk back violently. We quickly perceived the unmistakable cause: The word 'good' (always a questionable term in Stan's lexicography) he had negligently combined with that other, (always) unacceptable word 'faith'—and, as the unavoidable result, Stan's very flesh recoiled at the shock.]

In time Stan recovered from this paroxysm and finished his thought: "Now, I will give you my diagnosis of that 'holiday-deficiency disorder' which so troubles you, and I have no doubt that my suggested course of treatment will show the superiority of my approach."

"Let me begin," Stan started, "by re-stating that predicament ... that quandary in which you have fallen. You have recently re-visited (at this seasonally-appropriate time of the year) several of those well-beloved

holiday classics, such as *It's A Wonderful Life*, and *The Night Before Christmas*, and even, perhaps, *Mr. Magoo's Christmas Carol* (you would be surprised how many important professional men and women harbor a secret affection for that bumbling, near-sighted embodiment of literature's most famous skinflint). Nevertheless, no matter how many times you return to those characters, scenes and events which (before) spoke so eloquently concerning the Christmas Spirit, you no longer hear that message. Scenes which once moved you no longer have any power to stir your emotions."

"Thus, you thought that by coming to our Village and hearing those old traditional stories in this place—where you might screen out any competing or distracting messages, and isolate yourself from any unsympathetic comments or criticisms—you might restore to them the power which they had."

"However, it should be clear to you by now that every aspect of our Village is absolutely hostile to what you wish. In truth, it is the very founding impulse of this Village that every venerated book of received wisdom, every school or tradition having its own 'truth' to tell, every modern, casual habit having its roots in ancient, pious ritual, is forbidden here. All these things, having in them some taint of that supreme, immortal, loving Spirit, we strive untiringly to suppress."

"Hence ... you have witnessed our new version of that 'Modern Cratchit Family Feast,' which—it must be evident to you—finds its greatest triumph in bringing together under one roof those typical familial 'types' consisting of 'exhausted mother,' 'unruly daughter,' 'irresponsible son,' and not forgetting 'slightly slutty sister' and 'absent dad.' In my story, I bring all these 'types' (or, if my superior artistic skill is ever recognized for the genius it is, these 'Dickens-sonian caricatures') together in a way which appeals to the reader as altogether human, natural and even commonplace. Yet, I do all this without allowing my narrative to be contaminated with any of those ancient infectious and pestilent contagions (by which I mean 'religious teachings, rituals or traditions') which so often contaminate such stories."

"Here, we have no use for such empty, artificial abstractions. We do not inquire (and, thus, do not come to any guilty conclusion) as to the motivation which animates any choice which anyone here might make. We only know the 'result.' We do not care about the 'why.'"

"If there is something which I covet, or someone whose favors I desire (or, to the contrary, something or someone who repulses me) then ... these feelings which I have (despite you call them "Sins" and give them numbers), we smile and wink hold that person blameless. These appetites, we know, are but the most persistent of those supernatural effluvia which rule our lives. They are, we know, not the 'will' or 'soul' by which you mis-describe these things, but only some intangible, transcendental emanations of our earthly form."

"And all the rest is but the predetermined outcome ... the unavoidable product of our rational, fact-based and scientific world in which we live. I ask you: Who is there who would question that mechanically-derived 'result' which we see is but the inescapable outcome of some well-described 'set of givens' upon which we allow only the forces of cold, hard, impersonal 'science' to operate?"

Stan raised his voice. "Here, there is no 'law' (as if I would ever agree that others might legislate any limit upon my appetites or desires). Here, there are no 'scriptures' or 'revelations' (as if I would ever forebear to

take what I want, or seize whom I covet, at the instance of any such dead and departed authority). Here, we respect only those who use their strength and wits to dominate the weak."

"Here, when you say 'pitiless' we say 'principled,' what you call 'remorseless' we call 'single-minded,' and what you would label 'cruelty' we recognize as no more than 'nature's way.' Any other voice—which would counsel tolerance, moderation or mercy—we silence at once, by whatever force is necessary."

"You see, Winston ..." I heard Stan start to say. But he abruptly stopped, as if he had momentarily lost his train of thought (or found it waiting in some station where he had not expected it to stop). He took some few, brief moments to gather his wits about him (and as I watched him, it seemed to me he suffered some profound embarrassment, as if he had been guilty of one of those Freudian slips in which he revealed some mystery which he prefers to keep secret—not only from others, but from himself, as well). But, having fallen down prostrate as the result of this slip, Stan quickly regained his composure (and his footing) and marched off in the same direction as before.

"I'm sorry," he said. "I apologize. I ... was reminded of another, similar lecture which I (under another pseudonym) delivered to some other lost and vulnerable traveler, whom I hope might serve as an example to you (if you know who I am talking about—though I doubt you do)."

My Guide Responds

"**Y**es, well," said my guide, "I am very well aware of what character from literature you briefly decided to 'channel,' and I can see why you might have made that mistake. Although you have been uncompromising in your efforts to eliminate from this Village all of the world's most honored scriptures, prophecies and holy texts, I also see that you do have here your own 'unholy books.' And I have no doubt that the book you were about to recite is one whose message you admire (if we observe only its shallowest, most superficial message)."

"But our friend, here," he said, motioning in my direction, "is no Winston Smith, and I see in our near vicinity no hungry rats in cages. Thus, if you want our friend to agree with you, you will have to use no more than your own considerable powers of persuasion—unaided by any lever, rack or other implement of coercion, as you would otherwise bring to bear."

Now turning in my direction, my guide began his response. "Stan has (unwittingly, I am sure) made my job easier." (Saying which, Stan's eyes fell in mortification.) "He has not only given us a story—*A Christmas Carol*—which reflects those characters, themes and motivations which he would have you adopt, he has even gone back into literature to find another, even more compelling and descriptive explication of his underlying purpose."

"So we ask, what would Stan have us do, this Christmas season? Why, it's obvious. Simply ... get rid of Christmas, itself! No more Christmas trees, decorations, feasts, apparel or parties. Nothing red and green, silvery, snow-covered or cozy. No gaily wrapped gifts, no Christmas cards, no eggnog, no visits to Grandma's house, no hand bells and kettles in the snow. No Christmas dramas, music or movies, no elementary school pageants, and no romantic mistletoe. You did, earlier, compliment Stan on his thorough-

ness and persistence (which we admit are laudatory attributes of his efforts, no matter how misdirected his goal may be). And I agree with you; having set his course in one direction, he will not vary from it in any way."

"Now, despite what you expect, I must tell you I do not intend to argue with Stan's approach. I applaud his efforts to 'simplify' the Christmas season (which I say, extending at the same time my grateful acknowledgment of that rustic author and philosopher who likewise saw much virtue in 'simplicity'). Stan wants us to be done with all those ... attractive distractions, those repetitious and misleadingly cheerful solicitations in praise of seasonal generosity (of the discounted, gift-wrapped and non-returnable variety). And I am fine with that."

"When we compare the original Dickens *Christmas Carol* to that version recently commissioned by Stan, there is no comparison. The first is infinitely richer, deeper and more satisfying. It gives us ... holiday dances, games and feasts that are nothing less than joyous—and we cannot imagine how anyone (anyone not in service to the 'Lord of Humbug') could wish these things away. But this does not make it 'better' or more 'true' than Stan's anemic, anorexic version."

"For once helpful when his intention was to mislead, Stan poses us this question: If we wish to find, again, that authentic Christmas spirit, would we set out, directionless, into some chaotic, holiday-themed wilderness of confusion, distraction and over-stimulation? According to him, we would not. And I agree."

"But, knowing Stan, we also know that his true objective was to obscure the path by which we might discover the authentic Christmas message. This he did according to a clever, two-part scheme."

"First, he counseled us to forgo all the usual trimmings of the Christmas season, and by this he pretended to eliminate only those distracting, non-essential surface details ubiquitous this time of year."

"But then, (the second step), Stan (unable to conceal his stingy and ungenerous character) declined to offer any value in its place! Having balled up all the world's tinsel and glitter into one festive agglomeration of wrapping paper, sticky tape and misplaced price tags, he refuses to take it out to the trash! He forces us to live with that sparkly, sticky mess till New Year's Day! (And thereby causes us to miss the true meaning of the Christmas story.)"

My guide lowered his voice. "I ask you now: Recall that first Christmas morning. What do you see? An innocent, newborn child (the Son of Man, we know) born into that crude and humble dwelling, His birth unaccompanied by any grandeur, adulation or solemnity. His unadorned, unblemished flesh (exposed, as He was, to the gaze of animals, poor men, and travelers) teaches us but one lesson: That mercy and forgiveness are to be found only in spirit, never in its outward show."

"Behold! The Son of God! Sheltered with common beasts, breathing in with His first breaths the odor of fodder, straw bedding and dung. What does He show us but that He does not forebear to join His perfect spirit to that same weak and wasting body which we so protectively esteem."

"Thus I say! Take care! Attend unceasingly to that spirit which you are. Do not be deceived! Do not think that what you see – of flesh (that perishable, outward show) - has any truth or wisdom in it. Look for that only in spirit; look for that only with your heart."

Breaking the Rules

We sat in silence for a few moments, then I said, "I agree with you, Stan, the Village is not the place to try to rediscover the 'true meaning of Christmas.'" Then turning to my guide, I offered, "Still, I appreciate your efforts, and perhaps there may yet be some subject which is best investigated here, where we need not suffer that 'contamination' which Stan described."

Stan immediately spoke up, "Yes, it was delightful to have you visit us, and I hope that what you learned here will nourish your imagination and feed your ego. My only other hope is that—you having had your fill—we will not see you here again soon." Saying which, Stan brushed some crumbs of jelly donut off his sleeve and gave me a look as if to say, "Next time you come here, it will not be that detestable Tiny Tim whom we isolate in indefinite detention. The man asked, 'Are there no prisons?' and my answer is: 'I will show you!'"

Now, before continuing with my story, I must pause to remind the reader of my situation in the afterlife. I am here, as I speak, properly naturalized as a full-time citizen and resident. In one earlier and more lengthy account of my travels in the afterlife, I was privileged to be granted a kind of "temporary visa" permitting me to see and learn those things which would be of value to me in my few remaining years of life. I did learn many important lessons, which had the most profound and life-altering effect. Then, in time, like every other man or woman, my senses began to dim, my body weakened, and my formerly keen mind abandoned focus, becoming more and more indifferent to the world. Then, in the end, there was but memory, and after that I immigrated here.

So arriving once more upon these "pebbled shores," I was met again by my guide, whom I knew well, and whose wisdom and consideration I admired. It was his job,   once again, to give me a little lecture on the "Do's and Don'ts of the Afterlife" Do: Go back and find out where you lost your keys. Don't: No fair haunting people you didn't like. Do: If you want to go back and see your high-school rival for the honor of being Homecoming Queen (that stuck-up bitch who didn't deserve to win) that's OK, but only if you just want to see how much weight she gained. Don't: No matter what he offers you ("still, it's always nice to be rich"), promises you ("you'll never miss it") or (how cheap) he'll let you "take it off his hands," never, ever enter into any bargain with Stan.

There are some other rules, but for our purposes, now, there is one rule which caused me considerable anxiety. My guide told me, upon my arrival, that while I would be permitted to consult that "Celestial Archive" to see people, places and events of long ago, I would not—at least for some possibly lengthy "period of adjustment"—be allowed to revisit any persons, places or events of my own life. This means, all spouses, children, friends, (enemies), in-laws, grandparents, teachers, co-workers and so forth.

In explanation, my guide told me that, these people and events being so fresh in my mind, I would—if I were to spend time with them—soon be caught-up all over again in those very conflicts and challenges which it was one purpose of my death to see me leave behind. As well, inasmuch as those friends and family are still actively and authentically living that one life of which they are possessed (or, the "current one," at

least) my mere presence (though but spectral and intangible) may (or has been suspected to) influence them in some way. Thus, I was absolutely forbidden to see my children, or my other family.

Now, I confess to you, dear reader, that this one, seemingly reasonable rule was one I could not abide. It was beyond galling that I was free to become a silent, ever-present witness to the day-to-day domestic comings-and-goings of ... the Romanovs, Thutmose II, and Elizabeth Regina, but I was prohibited from attending even a common birthday party for one of my daughters. Does that seem fair? I did not think so.

Thus, some time ago, before the Christmas season had begun, I schemed and puzzled how I might overcome this ... what I considered "un-natural" and even "punitive" restriction. My guide, I knew, would not make an exception for me. (Note to self: Look up origin of phrase "goody two-shoes" in Celestial Archive.) However, I did know someone else who, if being asked to break a rule, will only ask, "Are you sure you only want to do it once? I could do it again, if you want." Yes, I am thinking of our host, who at this moment is eagerly awaiting my permanent departure from the Village, after which he will deny to one and all that I was ever here.

We three stood and prepared to say our goodbyes, and my guide (showing some excess of polite gratitude for the efforts of our host) picked up the empty coffee cups and set off in the direction of the counter to return them. It was at this instant that I knew I had to act! Now was the time, and I could not delay!

I looked Stan directly in the eye and begged, "Look, I know you want to get rid of me, but I have another problem which only you can solve. I don't know if you would be willing, but it involves breaking a rule." (Stan's eyes lit up!) "Let me propose this: I will leave now, but I will return—alone—in an hour, and if you think you might be willing to hear me out, and decide then if you will help or not, that would be much appreciated."

My guide did, that instant, return to our little group, but Stan (looking at me with a not very well-disguised conspiratorial look on his face) said, "Yes, yes, I will agree to that. Now, the two of you need to be on your way." Then pointing in that direction which would bring us most quickly to the border of the Village, he said, "Now off with you." (After which he stood there—watching—until he was sure we had gone.)

We began walking, and my guide at once challenged me, "What was that Stan was saying about a bargain?" (My guide was, in many ways, responsible for my welfare, and my being party to a conversation with Stan in which one of us used a word suggesting that some "bargain" had been reached, this fact could not but set off warning bells and flashing lights in my guide's little control tower of watchful observation.)

I had to think fast. My guide was not stupid, and even I knew that Stan was dangerous and not to be trusted. Nevertheless, I could not go back now. I said, "Well, I told him, if I ever hear another version of *A Christmas Carol* that I think he might enjoy, I will send it to him, if he will promise to read it. So, I guess he'll read it, if I ever come across such a thing." My guide seemed to be satisfied with my explanation, and he dropped the subject.

We walked awhile. Then, coming to the border of the Village, we parted, my guide taking the path which followed along the little river they have in the Village, going downstream in the direction of the bridge. As for me, I went in the other direction, going upstream in the direction of the pastures I had seen there before. But … I dallied, looking over my shoulder from time to time to watch the progress of my guide. When I saw that he had gone out of sight, I immediately turned around and retraced my steps to the border of the Village. After that, it was a short stroll back to the very table we had occupied in the coffee shop. I saw, as I neared the place, that Stan already there, waiting.

My Plea

I took my former seat across from where Stan was sitting. Knowing how much Stan wanted me to leave (or, more worrisome, how ready he was to have me work off the value of the coffee I had consumed by some lengthy, involuntary visitation to the Village workhouse), I hastened to make my pitch.

"On a thumbnail, Stan, the rule I want to break is this: I want to see my children and one other family member. I just want to see them … and, hopefully, to know that they are all right and going on with their lives in a healthy way. For all I know, one of my daughters has fallen ill, or lost her job, or been divorced, and, if any of that is the case, I want to see if she will get over it and move on with her life. I know I'm not allowed to communicate with them in any way—and I am not asking to break that rule—but, what I want is, I want to observe their lives so that I can put my own mind at rest. That's what I want."

Stan pondered for a moment, then replied, "That's not such a serious rule to break. Are you sure you wouldn't prefer something a little more … vindictive? Perhaps you would like to inflict a period of 'bad luck' on some former romantic rival who (you can never forget) stole the woman you loved? Something like … you know, repeatedly locking his keys in his car, dropping his smart phone in the urinal, cancelling all his credit cards for no apparent reason, spilling his Mochaccino all over his Ferragamos? I could arrange that."

I (hesitantly) answered, "No." (Not out of any actual indecision, but rather, in order to give Stan the impression that I had genuinely considered his offer.) "I would be perfectly happy simply to … 'observe.' Actually, I cannot think of anyone who, in my opinion, deserves to be haunted by a spirit practicing only so much evil as we would call it merely 'annoying, inconvenient, bothersome and slow.' Any more evil than that, and I would judge myself at fault."

"All right then," responded Stan, "we will limit ourselves to 'observer status.'"

"Well," I began, "there are four persons I wish to observe: my three daughters and my sister. I assume that my observing, for example, the children and spouses of my daughters will not create a problem? I really can't avoid seeing those other close family members at the same time. In addition, if one of my daughters goes to school to pick up her own child, I cannot avoid seeing the other students, their parents, teachers and the like. So, is that a problem?"

"Any other time, that would not be a problem," Stan observed, "but you have to remember, we are breaking a rule. And under that rule—strictly interpreted—you are not permitted to observe any of those people." Stan paused, seeming to give the matter his deepest consideration. Then he continued, "But I suppose there is some virtue (he gave a sort of sneer, as if he found any amount of virtue—however small—to be something contemptible) in the fact that we are not going overboard

with some long list of people you want to observe. So … all things con-sidered, I don't think it will be a problem. You are, after all, only 'observ-ing.' Tell me, though, are these persons your entire family? Are there any others still alive whom do not wish to see?"

"This is my whole family," I replied. "My wife passed away several years before I did, and of course I am not yet permitted to see her, either. Although, when that day comes we will truly be reunited, and I will not be limited only to the status of some anonymous 'observer.' My parents passed away years before my wife, and her parents, as well, are gone. I have no other siblings, no ex-wife and no unacknowledged children (that I know of … although, perhaps you could tell me if I do?)."

"No, no," Stan quickly responded. "You were always careful. Or, more accurately, your several temporary partners each planned ahead (and, it seems, did not see in you so much prospect as a desirable husband as to arrange any well-timed and—for her—fortuitous pregnancy)."

Stan continued, "But before we get started, there is something I need to explain. I have agreed to assist you in observing those four indi-viduals you have identified. However, inasmuch as we are breaking a rule, we will not have that usual unlimited freedom which you enjoy when you are seeking answers in the Celestial Archive. What I mean is, when I take you back to see, for example, that birthday party for your daughter—which you alluded to—you can go there as 'you' but I cannot go there as 'Stan.' That would also be against a rule (albeit a different rule from the one you wish to disregard). I, as Stan, would be instantly discovered were I were to bring you to do your observation, and the jig would be up."

"Accordingly, here is what we must do: I will assume (seriatim) the roles of those three famous ghosts in *A Christmas Carol*. First I will take you back to one or more Christmases in the past (as you designate). Then I will take you to several current-day Christmas celebrations involving the four persons you wish to observe. And, finally, I will take on the robes and demeanor of that third ghost, the one having the power to show you some few Christmases which your children and family may celebrate in the future."

"Thus, when we begin our travels, you will be granted the same privileges and capabilities that Scrooge enjoyed when he was traveling with his ghosts. That is, you will be invisible to those you observe, and you will be permitted to move about the room or other location you are visiting, so that you might see and hear all of the words and activities which you witness."

"Finally, and of most importance, when I take you to observe some one daughter, or sister, we must take care to observe her when she is involved in some Christmas-related activity. It must, in every case, represent some pastime essential to the Christmas season, as experienced by that person. In this way you can break your rule—and celebrate the season—at one and the same time."

These limitations did not strike me as any severe restriction upon my plan, so I readily told Stan that all was fine with me. He replied, "Good. We have agreed on that. Now, let us start by you telling me about your daughters."

I Introduce My Daughters

"All right, good," I began. "I start with my eldest daughter, Amelia. She was—honestly—always my favorite. I know that as a parent, I am not supposed to have a 'favorite,' and I did try my best to treat all my daughters equally, and never to favor one over the others. And I believe—speaking now strictly as a father—that I was successful in that regard. However, what the authors of all those parenting books (who warn you not to 'play favorites') often forget is that we parents each have our own personality and character."

"I am a lawyer and now looking back, I can see that I thought like a lawyer, and had the interests and human qualities of a lawyer, even in childhood—years before I went to law school or passed the bar. So later, when Amelia came along, she was so much like me in so many ways that we could not help but develop a special bond. My other daughters I love like … 'daughters,' but I will never share with them that same attitude toward life and work and family that Amelia and I share."

"Starting early in childhood, Amelia was the most studious of the three. She got good grades, good test scores, and was active in several high school clubs. She got into a good college, majored in English, and went on to become a lawyer. She got married coming out of law school and—last I know—had one child, a girl named Cynthia. You will not find anywhere a more accomplished, loving and responsible lawyer, wife and mother."

"My second daughter is Brittney. She was always the artist of the family. She took piano lessons and became very accomplished. She tried her hand at drawing and the visual arts, and produced some beautiful, life-like sketches. She ended up dropping out of college, but she made up for it by founding a sort of combination art gallery/coffee shop/comedy club/concert stage and organic restaurant, each and all of which are popular with the college students and young professionals in her neighborhood.

She got married—finally—after running through so many boyfriends that her mother and I gave up learning the names. But it was worth the wait. Her husband is a gem; he's so supportive, pitching in to do his share of raising their son, Michael. The boy would be—I am guessing—seven years old by now."

"Last, but by no means least, is my daughter Catherine." I was ready to go on, but Stan interrupted. "I don't mean to break your train of thought, but I have to ask, if you and your wife had had a fourth child, what name would you have given him or her?"

"Oh! Great question!" I enthused. "If a girl, she would have been 'Deborah' or perhaps 'Dorothy,' and if a boy, either 'David' or 'Douglas.'"

"Yes, well," Stan observed, "if every couple thought the way you and your wife did, the race of 'Stephanies' would be extinct, and those species classified as 'Megan' and 'Natalie' would be on the endangered list. In any event, you and your wife stopped at three, so we need not speculate what you would have done had your daughter 'Zuleika' suddenly acquired a younger sister."

"Please go on," Stan reminded me.

"Yes, Catherine, she is a dynamo! She was always the athlete of the family. She liked outdoor sports—rollerblading, snowboarding and distance running. But her energy didn't only show up in sports. She was always coming up with some elaborate, complicated plan for a fun (but challenging!) activity, and then (with her infectious energy) she drew everybody in to follow her lead. Her laugh, her sense of humor, and her unfailing solicitude for those around her, are simply amazing. She is a force of Nature!"

"Now, Catherine did finally graduate from college after taking a couple of unavoidable sabbaticals from her studies—one to deliver daughter No. 1 (Hope) and the other to bring into the world daughter No. 2 (Charity)."

I could see that there was something troubling Stan. Then, remembering what I had just explained, it came to me. "I can see the look in your eyes, Stan, and I know what you are thinking. However, I want to reassure you that it was Catherine's interest in family genealogy which provided her that list of historically resonant examples from which she and her husband selected her children's names—not some obscure Bible verse of which no one would be better off to be reminded."

My Sister

"So those are your daughters. Fine." Spoke Stan. "Now tell me about your sister, Connie."

I was brought up short. I felt, for the first time, a little of thrill of fear, to be here, alone, with Stan. I was immediately reminded of that longer, more proper name by which Stan is generally known outside the Village. That name did not trip joyfully off the tongue.

"How is it, Stan," I gently inquired, "that you know the name of my sister? I do not recall ever mentioning it." Then giving me the blankest of blank looks, he replied.

"Actually, I have some prior experience with your sister. The fact is, you know your wife came here—to the afterlife—several years before you did. Apparently, shortly after arriving, she began inquiring into your sister's welfare, but, like you, she was prevented from observing any persons from her life. Then … she came here. And I spoke to her. It seems she was concerned that your sister might have been the target of a few of my little 'jokes' (I like to think of them this way, though you may disagree) by which her feelings might have been a little hurt, or her spirits may have gotten a little bit deflated, as a result of some things I did. But really, how am I supposed to know how someone else is going to react to some harmless little tricks I want to play?"

"Well, what did you tell her?" I demanded. For once, Stan looked a bit chagrined, as if he feared to rouse my anger.

"I told her," Stan lied, "exactly what I would tell you—or any other person in her position. That any communications which I have had with your sister are strictly between us, and I do not answer to any other person for any grievance which you imagine she may have. That's what I told your wife, and what she said to me in reply, I will not repeat (though, in my opinion, it is a poor curse that does no more than seek to banish me to my own natural home and place of refuge)."

I sat silent, trying to puzzle out what was my best course of action—taking into account this self-evident lie which Stan had not been too embarrassed to tell me to my face. I calculated: I know he's lying; he knows I know he's lying; I know he knows that I know he's lying; he knows that I know he knows that I know he's lying. At this juncture, my analysis of the situation receded into that vanishing point at infinity, and I decided that what I really wanted was to be rid of Stan. And, since completing my observations seemed my best hope of doing so, I moved on.

"Very well," I returned to the subject. "Let me tell you about my sister, Connie. Though you claim to know her, I am sure you do not know her the way I do."

"My sister, Connie, is two years younger than me. Thus, we grew up close in age and developed from the first a close and sympathetic relationship. Now, Connie is one of those rare individuals who have a sort of hidden 'disability.' She was sweet and meek, and when she got older, she loved dolls and colorful dresses and dancing in her frilly little polyester ballet costume. She was, however, burdened with one notorious physical defect, of which the chief harm it did was to periodically send her into hiding (in her closet, with the door closed, crying). You see, Connie is one of those rare souls who are born into this world inhabiting a body of the opposite sex. She was born with all the outward aspects (and embellishments) of a 'brother' while in her heart she glowed the perfect 'sister.'"

"Connie did not have an easy childhood. Her natural talents and enthusiasms only got her into trouble, and on those occasions when she just 'gave in' (her spirit having been worn down with the burden of it all) and pretended to be the boy she was not, she wasn't very good at it, and convinced no one. On my side, I loved her, and we had a wonderful childhood. Those most satisfying games we played together did not depend on teams divided 'pink' from 'blue.' Her smile was always unashamed and would have brightened a face of either gender. We were always happy to be 'family.'"

"At our house, this problem with Connie was soon to solve itself. Our mother decided that—whoever or whichsoever she was—Connie was a treasure. She loved to play dress up, she loved to help her mother in the kitchen, and she loved to sit on her mother's lap and have stories read to her. What mother is there who, having suffered so much to bring her child into this world, would name that tiny body 'wrong' (as if it came to her in any way imperfect, or scorned by God)? So our mother allowed Connie to be "Connie,' and when there were problems or explanations to be made at school, she found a way to muddle through."

"Of our father, the story is shorter. By the time Connie had reached the age of six or so, he had become very much embittered. As, why should he be punished (for doing what?) by having such a son! And then his wife making everything worse by taking the boy's side ('What, just because the little freak is six years old?'). He took the car one night, and we never saw him again."

"When she got older, Connie finished high school, and then going on to the local night school she picked accounting as a profession. In time—I am proud to say—she earned her license as a Certified Public Accountant. That is how she has supported herself to this day (I assume), and she has had many grateful clients who trust and depend upon her good judgment. So ... Connie has earned her way through life, and she has never been the object of any charity—not any financial charity, anyway."

"Of her private life, I am not so well informed. She was ... she is ... a larger person than you would normally expect to see in a woman. She has still that male body in whose shame she arrived in this world, and I would not tell the honest truth if I said she showed herself a shapely, womanly body, or a feminine face, or any seductive female enticements. I do not remember her ever going out on a real 'date.' She had friends, mostly other girls her own age, and she participated eagerly in those frequent, high school mysteries wherein one of her female classmates asked

(of some unsuspecting but eligible male classmate) 'who is it "likes" him?' and being told the name, Connie and her friends would spend their idle hours upon that single, vital question: 'does he "like" her back?'"

"But, as I say, I never saw Connie have a date. And so, protectively, her big brother (me) made it my purpose to be a support to her, and to include her in my group of friends. And when we had parties and gatherings and 'big events' at our home, I always made sure to invite Connie. She never missed a one that I remember."

Having reached this place in my story, I stopped talking, as my throat was seizing up and would not obey my speech, and I had to give it time to find itself again.

The Ghost of Christmas Past

"**V**ery enlightening, I am sure," responded Stan. "Your sister is indeed an unusual person, and I can understand why you would have concern about her welfare. Nevertheless, we are here to do some 'observing' in a 'Holiday Greetings' kind of way, so I do not think we have any more time for someone who cannot make up her mind" (and then beneath his breathe, he added "or her body"). I came very near, at that instant, to assaulting Stan, but my overriding desire to be quit of him overcame my anger, and I reluctantly held back.

"We need to decide 'where' and 'when' and 'who' in some past Christmas that you wish to see. I must begin my ghostly impersonation with the Ghost of Christmas Past, so perhaps we could go back and see some more-or-less typical Christmas morning at your home; one involving not just all three children, but your sister, as well. Then, once we have spent a little time there, we can embellish that picture of each of your daughters by adding detail."

My anger had nearly cooled, and his suggestion did appeal to me. I replied, "OK. Let's do that." Then, searching for some basis upon which to declare one Christmas morning "best," it came to me. I would pick out that one Christmas morning when my daughters received those presents which they most reminisced about in later years. Thus I began picking through the years, which conveniently sorted themselves in this way.

There was that year of "games." And then that year of Brittany's fashion doll: the little plastic house, the sports car, the stable (including horse), the complete wardrobe, and the pose-able (and disposable) boyfriend. And going on, the year of "educational toys." No. That was a disaster. They opened the presents, figured out what was inside, and immediately went back to playing with those little plastic flying ponies (which—being kind, sweet and forgiving—do have much to teach us.)

Finally, I picked one year. I said, "All right, Stan, I picked a Christmas morning. It was the morning Catherine got her rollerblades. I can't place the year by the calendar, but I remember that morning, and I think all the girls got something memorable. So, that's the one I want to see."

At once, Stan leaped up. "Good! Let's go. I know which Christmas that was, and if you are fully prepared, we will go to it at once." I took a deep breath and said only, "Fine." Then I stood up, so that Stan could do what had to be done to take us to that time and place.

But before I could move a muscle, I was struck dumb: Shocked and astonished! Stan's entire appearance had changed! No longer was he "Stan" as I knew him. Now, the man I saw before me was attired in what

I can only describe as a chaotic hodge-podge of ill-fitting, mismatched and garish holiday accoutrements apparently patterned after one of Santa's more lurid nightmares.

On his head was one of those old-fashioned stocking caps which (in the years of *The Night Before Christmas*) men and women often wore to bed. However, this stocking cap appeared to be made of gold lamé, and had glued all over it variously-sized colorful fake jewels and diamonds, of which (as Stan turned his head) several immediately fell off onto the floor (as if he wore a cap made of sheepdog, and that breed being in a perpetual state of shedding and molting, Stan left behind him a trail of colored gems, glitter and stray pieces of tinsel).

Going further down his body, I saw that Stan wore the most appalling Christmas sweater I have ever seen. Across his chest I could make out two grossly misshapen images—one of Santa, and the other Rudolph the Red-Nosed Reindeer. Where others might capture these two iconic symbols of the Christmas season smiling and laughing and joyfully preparing to bring toys to little girls and boys, these two were pictured locked in mortal combat, of which Santa—wielding a large filleting knife—was clearly winning. In the background I could see one of Rudolph's sleigh-mates hung up by his heels in preparation for the Christmas Feast—to be carved into steaks and roasts to feed this hungry Santa.

Now, below his waist, Stan wore a pair of casual, comfortable corduroy pants of which the left side was red and the right side green. Then over-all was a regular, repeating pattern consisting of little white designs in the form of dollar signs ("$") and other such symbols of negotiable currency (Yen and Pounds and Euros and Yuan). (Later, Stan explained to me that these symbols were in honor of the widely-practiced Christmas tradition of gifting "money" to any recipient whom the giver knows is certain to return whatever present he or she receives.)

To finish out his outfit to best effect, Stan wore on his feet enormous, garish elf-slippers festooned with sleigh bells, so that his every step brought to mind that ancient, prophylactic practice known as "belling the cat." I thought, "How appropriate" though I did not share this observation with Stan, who, being costumed in this festive disguise, was now prepared to lead me on to have my wish.

Christmas Morning Past

He waved his hand, and immediately we were transported to the living room of the home which Molly and I shared. It was Christmas morning, but as yet no one had come down to see the tree—or that multitude of cheerfully-wrapped presents which (overnight) Molly and I had brought out of hiding and distributed around the base of the Christmas tree. Stan and I stood off to one side next to the bookcase, where we would be out of the way of those opening presents but able to see everything and everyone to good effect.

I hardly had time to get my bearings and check out the tree when all Christmas (!) broke loose! My three daughters rushed down the stairs and up to the tree, where each daughter commenced a rigorous investigation of the package labels to see which presents belonged to her. There were cries of "Wow! I know what this is!" and "This better be what I think it is!" and (after the elapse of no more than thirty seconds), "Is this all there is?"

Shortly after the arrival of the three girls, I saw Molly and I come in the room. Each of us was wearing no more than a robe over our pajamas (so great was our hurry to get downstairs, as we knew we could not allow the girls to be alone with the presents for any length of time). However, while I kept watch, Molly slipped out to the kitchen to start the coffee and put some sticky rolls in the oven to heat. We could not be expected to endure so much impatient and acquisitive Christmas cheer as these small children could produce, without the necessities of life. Thus we prepared ourselves to watch the carnage begin.

It was at this moment that the doorbell rang, and Molly went to let Connie in. It was her, right on time, and wearing her warmest (and only) coat. I saw myself greet her, and being given my instructions (in sotto voce), I slipped on my boots and went out to her car. There in the back seat I saw multiple, gaily wrapped presents, each prominently marked with the name of one of my daughters. I brought these in and took them into the living room, where their arrival produced another peel of shrieks and cries, "Wow! Is that for me? Look at them!" And to Connie, "Did you bring all these?"

Now, I watched the events of this Christmas morning with grateful recognition, seeing my daughters opening presents which gave them great joy, and observing, again, those characteristic habits which so exemplified each girl.

Amelia would open each present carefully, so as not to damage it with too much energetic gripping, ripping and stripping. Then studying the package exterior (until, by some unfailing psychic connection, she thought she knew what it was), she would consult her feelings to decide how she felt about it. Next, she would actually open the package, but would do so silently, as if fearing to allow some improvident remark to escape her lips before she was absolutely ready to pronounce sentence. When the foregoing preparatory formalities had been accomplished (and never before!), she would turn to the giver (either "Santa" or "Connie") and express her well-modulated gratitude.

As for Brittany, her style was different. She would take hold of the present, and (assuming it was not too large or heavy) she would hold it up in the air in front of her and turn it over and around. Then if she were so moved, she would shake it vigorously (as if, if she could only shake it hard enough, it would call out and confess its contents, rather than suffer any more violence). Or, alternatively, from time to time Brittany would engage the giver in an impromptu game of "Twenty Questions," in which she would attempt to guess the likely contents, repeatedly asking the giver "Did I get it right yet?"

Only after several of the family had had enough of this unnecessary and self-indulgent delay, and voices had been raised in injured exasperation, did Brittany bestir herself to actually open the present. (She did this every time; and did not endear herself to her anxious, impatient sisters. Connie, however, thought this was the funniest thing—that someone so young could already feel the need to make the moment last.)

Third, there was Catherine, who was, to me, an enigma. There were times when she would grasp the present and rip off the wrapping paper as if some family of pet gerbils were trapped inside and running out of air. Other times—it seemed when she could guess the contents, and the gift was the answer to some childish, wishful prayer she had whispered—she would, without warning, stop altogether. She might suddenly decide she was thirsty and needed juice, or hungry and needed a roll with butter, or (once) that she had forgotten to feed her fish, and all charitable benevolences had to be suspended until those finny dependents had been provided for. So we could never be sure how much time Catherine would need to open any given present (and aren't they all), but in time she relented, and seeing the gift revealed, bestowed upon the giver her purest, sweetest smile, and usually said, "It's just what I wanted."

But I have been indulging my most precious memories. I must keep to the task at hand. You have heard the styles and customs adopted (generally) by each of my daughters, but now I must confine myself to this one Christmas, and those most memorable presents which were opened that morning.

Those Precious Gifts

Since I have already picked this particular Christmas morning according to what I remember Catherine receiving, I will start there. When all three girls had exhausted the charitable efforts of Santa (having opened every one that bore his signature), it was time to open those gifts which Connie had brought. (And, despite what you might imagine, considering two natural parents in the room, one of whom earned considerably more than Connie, it was a case of "best for last.")

Catherine seized the present meant for her and, pulling it toward her across the rug, seemed to have some sort of vision of what it was. This I can only assume, because Catherine thereupon stopped and announced she needed to be sure her gerbils had fresh water, and Christmas had to wait while we satisfied a rodent's thirst. Then returning, Catherine finished opening the package and found what she had guessed. It was a new pair of rollerblades, in exactly the style and color she had wanted, and—the best—packed in the box were several colorful stickers showing images of her favorite flying ponies, such stickers destined to appear on the sides of her new skates.

You see, it was the practice of my sister, Connie, that on weekends, on Friday or Saturday evening, she would take Catherine (and often Amelia and Brittany, as well as several of their friends), to the local roller rink. There they would skate round and round, gossiping, laughing and making ever-more-frequent visits to the snack bar, where Connie maintained a "tab" for the evening which (I am pleased to say) was successful in forestalling that starvation, thirst and virulent sugar deficiency which so afflicts young rollerbladers.

Connie, herself, brought her own skates, and she happily skated round and round to the music, doing the Hokey-Pokey, the Chicken Dance, and enthusiastically waving her arms in just the right way when the DJ played "YMCA." But skating was by no means the most physically demanding activity which occupied Connie at the rink. No, far more challenging were those tasks (which only she was there to take on) which began with helping Catherine and the other girls lug their skate bags into the dressing room, then helping each girl fish out her skates, put them on (over multiple pairs of socks), and, finally, lacing up each girl's skates with just that amount of tension in the laces which … were any more to be applied, all circulation in that foot would be absolutely extinguished.

Then at the end of the evening, Connie was there to help each girl take off her skates and stuff them back into the appropriate skate bag (a task which she never omitted—not after that one night when one girl went home with two left skates, and another girl with two rights skates).

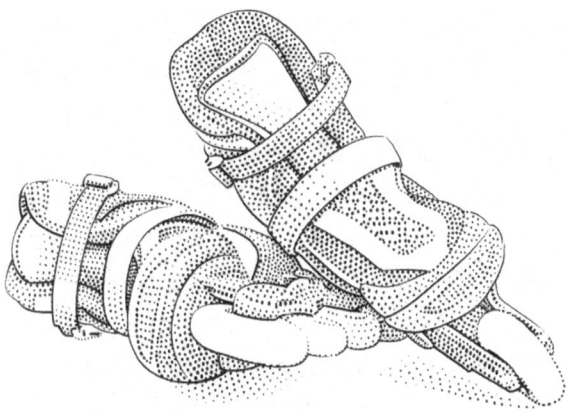

Finally, before herding her frolicking, flocking, feminine felines out to her car for the ride home, she announced "last call" at the snack bar, after which it was Connie's duty to settle her tab—reserving, always, one rapidly-melting ice cream sandwich for herself for the drive home.

Thinking back, now, on those many evenings which Catherine spent skating round and round, absorbed in the music and protected (briefly) from the cares of the world, I can see she grew in maturity—enjoying the music, the activity, and the sense of having so much bounty in her life that she could share it with her friends, and feel she gained more than she ever gave away.

My next daughter to open a present from Aunt Connie was Brittany. Here, I noticed that as Brittany picked up the gift and turned it this way and that, Connie appeared nervous, anxious and unsure of the result. Would Brittany like it? Did she guess right? I could see how she had agonized over her selection, and now was zero-hour! Brittany—mercifully, this once—laid the package down in front of her and—without any further ceremony—began to remove the wrapping paper, which in the case of this particular present, she did as if she were defusing a bomb. Upon hearing that she didn't need to "save the paper," she relented and just ripped the darn thing open.

It was a wooden box having a clever brass latch, and upon being opened, the box revealed a rainbow-like array of chalk pastels, each carefully and individually wrapped (like so many sugar candies) to keep their colors fresh. It was a thing intended for a true professional artist, of whom (that year) Brittany dreamed to be. And presently, Molly noticing an unopened envelop wrapped together with the chalk, Brittany opened it and found her most unexpected gift. It was a receipt showing that tuition had been paid for one "Miss Brittany" to enroll in a course called "Life Study" at the local community college. It was for the semester to begin with the New Year, and was to meet in the designated studio in the Art Building three times a week, from 6:00 to 8:00 pm.

This official document being read out by me (my robe-clad self), Connie at once volunteered that Brittany would need someone to drive

her there, and wait for her outside, and then drive her home, and she (Aunt Connie) being from childhood a patron of the arts, would consider it a great favor if she could be allowed to provide this little service in the greater purpose of supporting and propagating the finer arts. This offer was at once accepted. Brittany, over the course of that semester, refined her art and felt herself of special worth that by her passion, empathy and vision, she was able to preserve on canvas so many flattering, colorful likenesses (as if sketched out in marzipan).

Finally, it was Amelia's turn. And here, I must insert an apology, accepting responsibility for behavior of which Molly and I have much guilt to bear. We learned, early in our child-raising years, that on a much anticipated and endlessly-delayed-getting-here Christmas morning, the amount of "patience" which any child could be expected to possess was strictly in proportion to age. Hence, we could not help but follow a "youngest-goes-first" rule Christmas morning. Thus (with all my apologies), Amelia always got her presents last.

I saw Amelia creep deferentially up to the package which all knew to be hers, and drawing herself up on her knees in front of it, she prepared to do what she must. [You see, at that time, Amelia was of the age when she suffered from a serious, age-related lack of self-confidence, and the undeniable fact that someone was giving *her* a *present* was—for her— evidence either of a serious mistake having been made (by the giver), or a cruel joke being played (on the recipient).] Nevertheless, after much vocal encouragement from her parents and sisters, she was finally imposed upon to do the deed.

She took off the wrapping and opened the box, and her expression at that moment I will never forget. She reached in, took out and held up

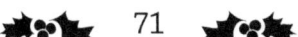

for all to see a pair of ballet pointes—used, and showing themselves old and worn and mended. Turning at once to her aunt, Connie assured her, "They belonged to that dancer you like. She was wearing those the last time we saw her." Amelia was touched, and I could see tears come to her eyes. Then Connie went on, "And, it's not in the box ... but I got us tickets to the rest of the season, if you want to go." Amelia allowed as how she would—not by words, which would not come to her, but only by her smile in Connie's direction.

You see, beginning earlier that year, and now arriving at the holidays, but destined to be extended for the whole next year and the following season, Connie had been pursuing her own version of what the music industry calls "artist development." She offered to Amelia the opportunity to see several local artistic performances of the cultural sort—being a ballet, a concert by the city orchestra, or even a classic stage-play. Upon Amelia accepting, she was (she learned) expected to accompany

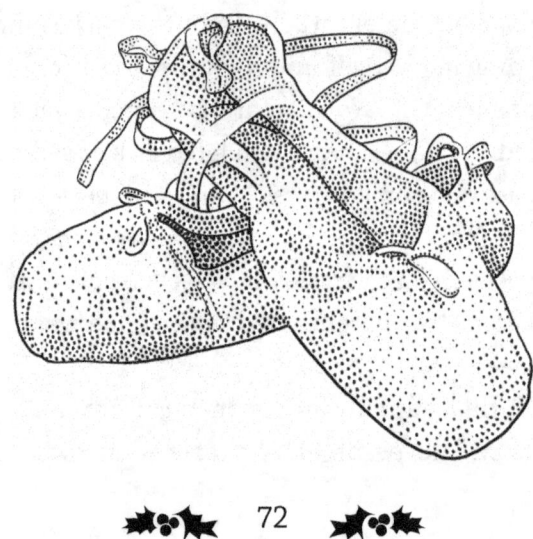

Aunt Connie to a pre-concert meal, which involved the two of them visiting a "white tablecloth" restaurant. There, Amelia was treated as the mature, sophisticated and self-assured young lady which Connie wished her to become.

Then on those occasions when the concert or performance finished early enough, Connie often declared that she could not hope to sleep unless she stopped by the local artists' coffee house and had hot chocolate or some of that fizzy Italian lemonade. There being no way conveniently to drop Amelia off at home on the way, there was nothing to be done but have her tag along to the coffee house, and nothing else for Amelia to do when they got there then to expound her own opinion of the performance, thereby educating Connie on the costumes, stagecraft and over-all artistic mood created by the performers (a process which usually could not be completed before the second round of beverages had been consumed).

"Yes, yes," Stan interjected, "I see that the fine arts owe some debt of gratitude to your sister, despite her (also) going into debt to finance those efforts. But unless I am mistaken, none of your daughters have had a career in the fine arts, so I cannot see the value in your sister's gifts. Nevertheless (though it hurts me to say this, as I do not like to encourage any unexpected acts of spontaneous forgiveness, even by those whom, I greatly suspect, do not hang upon my every word), 'Who am I to judge?'"

Although I did not like to have Stan provide the "final word" upon our visit to observe my family's Christmas Past, I also did not much relish getting into an argument with him about the appropriateness of his "summation." But feeling as I did that even his uncharitable elegy might, in the mouth of someone whose benign intentions are more to be relied upon, have its time and place—and serve His purpose—after all, I let it go.

A Respite

Stan waved his hand, and we were immediately returned to our place of departure. I wish I could say that Stan's clothing did not return with him, but, alas, it did. Here I had no choice but to look upon that sweater—unless I could somehow manage to keep my gaze fixed upon his hat (as if upon a "twinkling star"). However, my eyes involuntarily returned again and again to his sweater, so I had to find some other solution.

I held my hand up to my brow to shield my eyes from the sight, and asked him, "Is that what you are going to wear to impersonate the next ghost? Don't you think you ought to change your appearance to be the Ghost of Christmas Present Day?" (I was confident that, whatever change he might make to his apparel, he could not help but choose a less-offensive sweater.)

How naïve I was! And how forgetful of the endless creativity shown by Stan when his purpose was to do "wrong." Stan only smiled at me. Then again waving his hand, his whole appearance changed.

First, his hat was changed over to one of those springy headbands that anchor two large, multi-pronged fake reindeer antlers (in this case further wrapped with tinsel, so that there would be no question which holiday was intended).

His sweater was—mercifully!—gone, and in its place a sort of colorful holiday-blazer, being a jacket in the style of a man's sport coat, in red and green checkerboard material, but having the sleeves, the lapels,

the collar, the pockets and the button-holes all decorated with flashing, blinking, tiny holiday-lights, seemingly powered by a battery hidden away in Stan's pocket. (Which, considering the excessive number of lights, their piercing brightness and strobe-like intensity, can only have been of the "nuclear" variety.) His slacks were, I eventually determined, made of that same material from which those garish, outdoor blow-up Santas are constructed, but Stan showed his devotion to holiday tradition, too, by retaining his elf-slippers (including bells).

I felt a bit dizzy and lightheaded at this conquest of my senses by Stan's relentlessly overbearing holiday cheer. Thus I sat back down at the table in the coffee shop, and Stan joined me.

"I think we should rest a few minutes," Stan said. "There is something I want to be clear about before we go any further." I was silent, and let him go on.

"Our next ghost whom I must impersonate is the Ghost of Christmas Present Day. So I assume we will be traveling to … some more-or-less 'present-day' Christmas morning. But, of course, this will be a Christmas morning without you; and, it goes without saying, without your wife, the mother of your daughters. Thus we will observe all three of your daughters celebrating—together (if circumstances so permit)—a Present-Day Christmas in but one living room, and opening presents under but one Christmas tree. This must be what you expect."

He paused to see if I would object, and when I did not, he went on.

"Most importantly, you have insisted that you be permitted to witness your sister's holiday, as well. And I have agreed to satisfy your request. Thus, we will 'observe' how your sister, Connie (alone or in the company of others), celebrates the Christmas day."

"But before we go, I ask, are you prepared to see how time has changed the ones you love? It has been years since that Christmas morning made notable by rollerblades, pointe shoes and chalk. Years since even your youngest daughter became independent and moved out of your house. Years since your grandchildren were born, and years (eventful … and all unknown to you) since you passed away."

"All this being the case, what makes you so certain that … attending but the one Christmas morning, and standing in the glow of but one Christmas tree, you will observe not just your daughters, but your sister, as well?"

The Promise

"There did come a time," I responded, "when our happy little improvisational ensemble reached the limit of its run. Each of our daughters, one by one, either went off to college (never to return) or launched herself into self-reliance by moving out of the house. We had a few years when the girls came home at Christmas only if their college or work schedules allowed, and it was not too many years thereafter when spouses began to be accumulated. Then we reached the year when Molly passed away, and Christmas, for me (as well as for them), lost a good part of its luster. After that, I could see that the center (me) would not long hold."

"Thus, in that final year, that time when I and all my daughters and Aunt Connie could plainly see my final chapter ending, I had a little talk with each of them (my daughters only … only them).

"I asked each one to make one solemn promise, which was this: That in the years to come, they would remember my sister—especially at Christmas time. I asked each daughter to make some special effort to reach out to Connie in some expressive way, and bring her into their families' hearts, so that—on Christmas Day—she would not feel forgotten."

"It was my hope for Connie that, her older brother being gone, those daughters whom he left behind would keep his promise (notwithstanding death). It was that life-long pledge I made; to honor that love our mother showed for Connie. Since ... as Mom always said, "Christmas was made for little girls." And among them, Connie.

Catherine's Assignment

I could see that my description of the "promise" which I had extracted from each of my daughters made some impression upon Stan. He sat pondering, as he tried to incorporate this new information into his pre-existing picture of my Christmas Present Day. At last he spoke.

"Yes ... this explains a lot. Until this moment, I had not understood several, rather odd pastimes indulged in by your daughters. However, hearing of the existence of your 'Christmas contract,' and especially learning of its terms and obligations, I believe I know, now, where we should be going to show to you this 'Christmas Present Day.'"

Stan waved his hand, and (as if in response) the blinking lights on his jacket began to flash with ever-increasing rapidity, and with near-blinding intensity, until ... I recoiled in fear (!) sensing that they would soon reach that final, irreversible point of ignition (where I waited, helplessly, for the detonation). Instead, I found myself transported to our destination.

I looked around but did not recognize the place. There was a table in what seemed to be an ordinary, well-kept suburban kitchen. There were boots scattered willy-nilly in the general vicinity of the back door, multiple cell-phone chargers left plugged in to those two counter-top receptacles which are most urgently and critically needed to plug in vital kitchen appliances, and a colorful, jumbled, pulsating collage of photos stuck to the front of the refrigerator (which, if I looked too closely, seemed to change before my eyes).

Then, coming in the back door, I saw my youngest daughter, Catherine, accompanied by her daughters, Hope and Charity. Each carried or pushed or roughly dragged into the room a mammoth bag of groceries. Taken together, these bags represented what appeared to be a month's shopping for the necessities of life.

Meaning … they contained multiple boxes of hot breakfast cereal (to be mixed with water and appropriately nuked), multiple boxes of pasta casserole (not so much "pre-cooked" as "extruded"), servings of beef, chicken or turkey (gravy over), and vegetable side-dishes (invariably smothered with government surplus cheese)—all of the foregoing to be, again, appropriately nuked. Thus I could see that Catherine was one of those mothers who takes seriously her responsibility to teach her daughters to be "independent," and—this requiring them to know how to cook—she had wisely laid-in a full winter's provision of just those very dishes which she knew her daughters would grow up to subsist upon.

I waited patiently as Catherine and her daughters emptied out the bags and put their future meals away. Then the two young children ran off

to the playroom, and Catherine walked over to the counter to check the mail. Shuffling through the usual bills and ads, she found one large manila envelope addressed to her. Seeing this, she cried out in pleasure to see that it was from her sister, Brittany. At once, Catherine took the envelope over to her kitchen table; then reaching up into a nearby cabinet, she took out another, similar envelope, as well as a small loose stack of photos.

I started to walk over nearer to Catherine, so that I could see what she was doing, and have a better look at what appeared to be a stack of lively, candid photos, but Stan put out his hand to restrain me.

"No," he said. "You are close enough. You are permitted to observe your daughter doing what she will with those photos—editing, re-arranging and fawning over them—but it would not be proper for you, by your own skill and volition, to do that very thing which she intends."

I did not argue or press the issue with Stan. From his tone of voice, I could tell he expressed some admonition which did not originate with him, but which—at some previous time—he was constrained to obey. So, I stood there watching, but even without being impermissively close, I soon made out the task which occupied all of Catherine's efforts and attention.

I had already seen that one of the manila envelopes was from Brittany, and I soon guessed that the other was from Amelia. Of course, the stack of loose photos could only be those collected by Catherine, herself. I saw she made three stacks of photos (keeping them scrupulously apart), and then, setting two of those stacks aside, she turned her attention to the third. This she spread across the table top, moving the photos this way and that until it seemed she came to some attractive, expressive arrangement that pleased her. She then carefully divided that array of loose photos to produce what I gathered were the proper number of photos to be stuck upon two standard-sized pages of a common photo album. This she promptly did, filling up those two pages with at least a half dozen photos on each page, and keeping the pages in the order which she intended.

Having made remarkably quick work of the first pile of photos, I watched Catherine go on and repeat the same process with the other two piles. When she was finished, I saw she had seven pages of photos on the table top before her (Brittany could never edit herself). Then (and when she did this, my heart swelled in gratitude) she took a marker and wrote—carefully, but in letters large enough to be appreciated by some-one whose eyesight is not what it used to be—first, the name of the daughter (Amelia, Brittany or Catherine) whose photos were collected on the page, then next, the year, and last, the words "For Aunt Connie."

When Catherine finished the job, she put a small, light rubber band around the stack of album pages. Then, taking out from the cabinet another, larger envelope, she put it down on the table and addressed it to Aunt Connie, adding her own name and address as the return address. She next put all the pages in the envelope, sealed it up, and put it over by the house telephone where its large, manila-colored presence (so out of place in this marble and stainless steel kitchen) would no doubt soon remind someone (herself or, better yet, her husband) to take it down to the post office and get the right postage on it before it went out.

I looked up from where Catherine was sitting and caught Stan's eye. I felt that—as to this daughter—I had seen all I needed to see. Obviously, she and her sisters had come to some thoughtful, well-organized plan to keep Connie up-to-date with all three families, and (as I knew my girls would do) avoid any sisterly conflicts by sharing out the job equally

among all three households. I could see Catherine's job had involved what—from a distance—looked to be casual, candid snapshots of the members of each family. I could not help feeling proud to see this effort my girls had made to keep their promise and bring Connie into their warm, domestic scene.

Brittany's Assignment

Seeing me catch his eye, Stan waved his hand, and we were instantly similarly positioned (as to refrigerator, microwave and kitchen table) but yet standing in a completely different house. I looked around, hoping to see some photo on the wall (or, more likely, defacing some appliance) that would reveal to me whose home this was. However, before I could find any such photo, the back door opened and a well-dressed young man in his early 30's came in. I struggled to recall his face, but presently it came to me that this was Brittany's husband, Gary. He turned on the lights, kicked off his snow boots, and quickly left the room to go to the hall closet to hang up his coat. Coming back to the kitchen, he opened his briefcase and took out the family mail, throwing it on the kitchen counter where all such unsolicited intrusions (suspected of harboring propositions, supplications or demands of a financial nature) could be quarantined and—if possible—cleansed of any threat to human life or credit score.

We were in luck, and only moments after Gary left the kitchen Brittany came in. With her was her son Michael, who groaned under the weight and bulk of a costume only slightly less garish and monstrous than Stan's departed sweater.

Michael dragged into the room the pieces of his hockey goalie's gear, which he had been determined to bring home for the Christmas holiday. Brittany helped him with his burden thusly: She coached him, "Hurry up! Get inside! Close the door! Don't scratch the floor!" Following which, summoning all his strength (and no doubt inspired by the aforementioned cheerful encouragement of his supportive mother), Michael did succeed in bringing all of the components of his protective uniform all the way into the kitchen (far enough so that the back door absolutely, undeniably, could be all-the-way closed). Then running off to somewhere else in the house, Michael abandoned the whole of his goalie outfit right where it was until that day three weeks hence when it was time to go back to school.

Now, Brittany's actions in her kitchen were similar enough to Catherine's that I might have thought myself to be dreaming, and back-and-forth confusing one kitchen with the other. Brittany found her envelopes, made her little, loose stacks, and laid-out the pages one-by-one, just as her sister had done. However, by looking carefully, I discerned the vital difference in these respective stacks.

Each of Brittany's stacks seemed to be "headed" by one, tiny little photo, with some half-dozen (or so) larger photos displayed on the same page around and under it, as if for illustrative or explanatory purposes. Peering carefully, and sneaking up as close as Stan would allow, at last I understood the plan.

The tiny little photo was, in each case, one of those photos which all student sit for during the autumn of each school year. (You know, I think, that other, well-beloved "class photo" featuring the teacher and all her students in the class—which, according to binding contract with the photographer, always includes one shy child who is to be seen with his or her eyes completely closed).

But of more relevance, here, is that photo of the child alone, sitting cheerfully and guilelessly in possession of that hairdo which will ever-after set the bar for personal shame. Each child was (for a modest price) entitled to procure thirty or fifty or more copies of that little photo, to be handed out and traded with classmates. There were larger sizes for grandparents and others, but every child came away from the exercise (after all the trading had been done) with no fewer than thirty-eight pho-tos of himself left over (never to be traded, and destined to be part of his estate at death) and another twenty-five or so photos of his or her immediate classmates. This later group was to be looked at no more than once or twice—except, in the case of Michael, and every other boy, the photo of that one little girl who was his unforgettable "first crush."

So, I saw Brittany placing one of those little photos at the top of each album page, and I could only suppose that these were photos of the next generation—Michael in Brittany's family, Cynthia in Amelia's, and Hope and Charity in Catherine's. Brittany assembled the pages, applying the unavoidable excess of sticky, smelly glue, and then packaged up the pages as I had seen Catherine do before.

I felt as if that modest kitchen glowed with love, to think of Brittany laboring so dutifully—and so cheerfully—to assemble what all three sis-ters had contributed, and which—if my peering and surmising were cor-rect—could not help but bring a tear to Connie's eye.

Once again, Stan caught my attention, and I nodded my assent. He had concluded that I had found my time with Brittany productive, and that I no longer felt the need to continue my "observation" in her kitchen. He once more waved his hand (though this time, we were spared any dazzling, ever-intensifying countdown to destruction). We enjoyed a simple, uncomplicated transport to the home of Amelia, the only daughter I had not yet visited.

Amelia's Assignment

Now, since witnessing the activities with which I found Catherine and Brittany busying themselves (involving album pages of the sort universally destined to be included in some honored, studied and carefully-preserved family record), my fears had been considerably allayed. Where before I was not certain my promise was being faithfully kept, now having seen two of the three sister doing so, I could not doubt that Amelia would have her own part in this shared, sisterly gesture of inclusion.

I found myself standing in the corner of Amelia's study in her home. This was clearly where she came to do work at home. She had an antique wooden desk and a lamp having a lamp-shade in the style common in the 1920's (featuring a soothing, green-glass shade which served an illuminated emblem of trustworthiness, frugality and professionalism). She was that moment seated at the desk; the overhead light extinguished so that the screen of her laptop would be easier on her eyes, and convenient to her left hand was a can of soda sitting on a coaster.

I gave myself a few quiet minutes just to watch her work. I had not seen her since I came to the afterlife, and having her before me with all her familiar little quirks and habits was almost more than I could bear. Part of me wanted to speak up and ask her one of those questions to

which a father can never get a satisfactory answer from his daughter. The other part of me (the part that shrunk and cowered under Stan's ever-watchful scrutiny) knew that the best outcome I could expect would be merely to prolong this moment (by whatever subterfuge I could devise). My time was precious, and I dared not risk it all upon some deceptive misdirection that might easily be discovered (knowing that the greatest practitioner of that art stood at my elbow).

I did move up as close to Amelia as Stan would allow, and by looking over her shoulder I could read some of what she was writing. I assumed— since Stan had brought me to this moment—that it was something relevant to Christmas, and to that special promise involving my sister. As I read, I saw that this was so. By squinting my utmost, I could just read the heading of what she typed, and when I was sure I had read it right, my heart leapt up in pleasure!

It said "Connie's Christmas Newsletter," and I could just make out below that, in smaller letters, and serving as headings for additional text interspersed among the headings, the names of the months, beginning "January" and going on from there.

Though I could not read any of the words in smaller type, I felt that I could guess her plan and purpose: That she had earlier collected—and was now typing out—a month-by-month account of various newsworthy events, honors and accomplishments of both her own daughter and of Michael, Hope and Charity. Seeing this, I instantly understood how precious every "Christmas Issue" of this little periodical Newsletter must be to Aunt Connie.

In my imagination, I could easily picture Amelia reporting (someday) on Charity's attendance at her first Valentine's Day dance (including lengthy descriptions of the style and color of her dress, her nails, her shoes, her make-up, her accessories, her hair, and—if anyone can remember his name or what he looked like—one or two words about her date). There would, I am sure, be news of Michael's exploits on the ice, and on the grid-iron, as well as an account of his eventual elevation (by acclamation) to that glorious (and yet all-too-burdensome) office of Homecoming King.

Finally, when this promising younger generation reaches a more advanced age, I had no doubt my eldest daughter would be there to record (in some future edition of the Newsletter—to be read and re-read by Connie in the glow of some apply designed app), her most congratulatory accounts of high school, college and post-graduate graduations, and, on those occasions, I am sure, Amelia will take care to note any special "honors" awarded at each such ceremonial milestone; such honors, we know, being often accompanied by one of those lexicological appendices in the Latin language commemorating the achievement by the graduating student of that quality of "laude" which—in the opinion of the tenured faculty—has been so amplified, polished and improved by the efforts of the graduate as to be invested with an intangible aura of "magna" or—in rare instances—"summa."

Thinking of Amelia's task, there was no need to look for any manila envelopes in the mail. Amelia could easily flesh out a properly "newsy" newsletter merely by consulting all of her weekly or even daily conversations with her sisters—neither of whom was likely to keep any notable or publicly-recognized achievement by one of her children secret. Thus, Amelia had a wealth of material to share, and knowing that she made her living by putting a positive, upbeat "spin" on her clients' sometimes questionable behavior (when she wasn't pointing with alarm to some other lawyer's client, who was plainly a threat to public order), I knew she would do an excellent job of composing an amusing, readable and "true-enough-under-the-circumstances" newsletter for my sister's benefit.

I continued to watch Amelia for as long as I could, from time to time moving around the room as if I were seeing something on her screen of immediate, vital urgency, but at last Stan caught on to my game and motioned for me to get ready to go. I took one last, reluctant look at Amelia, seeing in her the (feminine) image of myself at the same age, and equally devoted to the law. At that, Stan waved his hand, and we were returned to the place from whence we came.

My Crime Discovered

Having arrived by the wave of a hand (and someone else's hand, at that), I did not feel in any way fatigued, and was ready to start off at once for our next destination. However, in but seconds I realized that things had changed. The table in the coffee shop was right where we left it, and I could not avoid being reminded (by the luminous presence to my left) that Stan was still there. But what made my stomach drop was this: I saw my guide sitting at the table, and he did not look happy.

Seeing my guide, Stan waved his hand, and his costume and appearance went back to "Stan." We stood silently, waiting for my guide to speak. During this interval, I was struck by how ... "clarifying" it was to my thought processes, to add this dash of "consciousness of fault." I did not rush directly to the consequences (I did not know what punishment might await, so I could not picture that dread result), but instead tarried awhile in that place where I regretted where I had begun, and wished to go back there and start again, and pictured myself arrayed in virtue, rejecting with utmost distain that temptation which got the whole thing started. Thus, I silently began to punish myself, hoping (thereby) to prove to my guide that any efforts of his along that line would prove redundant.

Stan, for his part, only looked around stupidly, ignoring my guide and feeling that any guilt he bore was nothing burdensome, and he could carry it around all day, for all he cared.

My guide, however, clearly seethed. His jaw was set, and he looked at me with poorly-restrained exasperation. If ever there was a facial expression that spoke the words "What am I going to do with you?" his was it. My guide lifted his coffee cup to his lips and, seemingly brought back to himself by the vapors, he glared down at it, whereupon it promptly turned to ice. I got the message.

"I am surprised, and I am disappointed," my guide began, looking at me. "It is not as if you have no familiarity with Stan, or his 'bargains.' How could you imagine that any good could come of this … breaking the rules? And enlisting Stan—of all people!—in your plan? In case it has not been made sufficiently clear to you before, Stan is not to be trusted. Yes. He is not permitted to outright lie to you, or to show you anything wholly 'false.' However (and this you know), nothing prevents him from showing you some plausible half-truth, or … some secret wish you have, dressed up in falsehood (which pleasing you, you never see the fraud), or even (with the collusion of your unconscious mind) some 'attractive illusion' misleading more by 'dream' than 'waking.'"

"And as for you!" he said, turning in Stan's direction. "You are forbidden to have any further contact with our traveler, here, until such time as

he has completed his period of adjustment and is fully released to travel freely about the afterlife. And before you open your mouth to make any rude comments, be assured you will not see him in this Village, again, until he is fully adjusted. Now, why don't you wave your hand and see if you can go fit yourself into a new sweater, one less detestable and lacking that aura of mockery by which, I gather, you strive to be considered 'transgressive.'"

I looked over at Stan, expecting to hear from him excuses, rebuttals or one of his impromptu histrionic performances reflective of his "injured innocence" (always a treat, as his attempts to simulate "innocence" were a sight to behold). However, in this case:

1. Stan knew he was wrong; we knew he knew he was wrong; he knew we knew he knew he was wrong; we knew he knew we knew he knew ... (and continuing this same pattern until everyone loses interest),
2. Stan didn't care, and
3. Stan had already given up his plan of seeing me confined in the Village workhouse.

Then ... he waved his hand, and he was gone.

My Guide Reproves

My guide being seated, and I standing before him in all my holiday-themed guilt (which could not be waved away), I considered it wise to remain standing, as (remembering every prison movie I had ever seen) that was the posture universally required of the prisoner. Moreover, I could not help but look down at my feet, as if searching for those tell-tale "blood spatters" (which, in this case, consisted of bits of tinsel clinging to my pants) which would mutely testify to my crime. I considered it no less than the beginning of my punishment, to stand silently and wait for my sentence to be announced.

At last my guide reached that final resolution of the struggle which occupied his inner-dialogue. It was a contest in which "Your punishment is to wear one of Stan's sweaters from now till Christmas Day." vied with "You will be designated 'Fruitcake Inspector of the Afterlife'—testing, sampling and certifying all available varieties thereof (and subsisting only on the same) till Christmas Day be done." I am the sort of person (lawyer, idolizing the law) for whom merely hearing that I may be made a public spectacle (my features clothed in guilty shame) would be punishment enough. No doubt I cringed, permitting that "consciousness of guilt" to briefly show itself.

Mercifully (as was his wont), my guide spoke up, "I have been watching you since that time when you told me that 'story' about how you were going to keep Stan up-to-date on new versions of the *Christmas Carol*. You are, if I may be blunt, a bad liar. Though your dishonesty pales in comparison with that of your companion, having him right there must have put me in the mind of 'subterfuge,' and thereby helped expose your little scheme."

"Look," I blurted out, "I'm sorry. I don't know what else I can say. There is no way I would blame this on Stan—it was my idea, and I'm the one who suggested it. I knew it was against the rules and, obviously, I went to Stan because I knew he would—maybe—help me get what I wanted. So, I don't know what the procedures are in this case, but if you need to impose some punishment on me, I accept it."

Once again, my guide got very quiet; and once again, I started to get nervous about what was going to happen. I did feel somewhat better, having made my confession, but even with my sincere acceptance of responsibility, there were, perhaps, factors at work here (of which I was unaware) that would nevertheless cause my guide to impose some actual, serious punishment upon me. All I could do—once more—was sit and stew.

At last he spoke, "If you did not understand the rule, or the reason we need the rule, I would have no choice but to impose some rather serious sanction upon you. However, I heard you (when you were speaking with Stan) give a good account of the purpose of the rule—and, of course, you being a lawyer, you well understand the application of the rule, and how you are undeniably guilty of breaking it."

"However, there is in this case a rather exceptional circumstance which leads me to impose, in this one instance, a 'consequence' for your misdeed which you may be surprised to hear. But first, you must acknowledge that one, pre-eminent fact which implicates the rule: You have witnessed your children as they exist today. That breaks the rule."

"I know," I whispered, "I'm guilty; I broke the rule."

"Good," my guide concluded, "We are done with the 'guilt or innocence' phase of your trial. Now, we must go on to the 'punishment phase.'"

"It is here that we come to that 'exceptional circumstance' which I spoke of before, and which we must take into account in your case. It is this: That in the afterlife, we do not permit any story to be 'continued later.' We do not allow our residents to be left in any state of 'indecision' or unresolved 'suspense.' We have found it is not conducive to 'virtue' to leave our residents to speculate upon the outcome of some moral dilemma (wherein it is only by the 'moral' choice, made rightly, and at the proper time, that evil might be avoided)."

"If I may provide a helpful, earthy metaphor to better explain myself: In my view, you have stolen a pie, and run away with it, and eaten half. Now, I will require of you that you consume the other half, then ask of you your judgment on the meal. If it be sweet and wholesome (then you must say); or do you purse your lips, and choke and gag, and call the thing a pastry baked of 'bitter fruit' that nourishes no one?"

"Thus, despite what you have been expecting, I am going to take over the role of Ghost of Christmas Present Day, and later, Ghost of Christmas Yet to Come, and take you to those places where Stan would have taken you, to see those things Stan would have shown you. This I do so that you may see the true outcome of those 'tendencies' put in motion in the past, which still lie dormant."

"I will show you those ... as yet unseen, unguessed and unimagined 'purposes' which, being cultivated over time (in some confused, conflicted heart), have not yet budded into that fruit which such branches are fated to bring forth."

Christmas Morning Rituals

My guide being ever as good as his word (duh), he forthwith stood up from his seat at the table and, waving his hand (Darn! I am going to try that one of these days!), we quickly found ourselves once more in a sub-

urban living room, shortly before dawn, but showing all the artificial light (and authentic Christmas glow) which "too-many" strings of Christmas lights provides. Looking around, I did not at first recognize whose living room it was, but seeing on the mantle a statue of "Lady Justice" (being that accomplished, degreed professional woman, attired in a flattering tailored robe, demurely blindfolded, and holding a balance scale—symbolic of her successfully balancing "motherhood" with "career"), I immediately concluded this must be Amelia's living room.

Once again, my ghostly guide had so timed our arrival that we materialized just moments before the first celebrants came into the room. Tumbling down the stairs and falling chaotically at the foot of the tree were three pajama-clad little girls. These I recognized (after some close study, it having been a few years since I had seen them) as Hope, Charity, and Amelia's daughter, Cynthia. They went straight for the stockings hung from the mantle, and after each child had delivered one, decisive irresistible tug to that stocking with her name on it, she had her loot. They commenced to play with the toys and games found in their stockings, and in a short time the next wave of celebrants appeared.

These were two couples, four adults, consisting of Catherine and her husband, Alex, and Amelia and her husband, Mark. Before coming down, each had hurriedly slipped into comfortable pajama pants and a Christmas sweater that, while colorful and gay, would have been flatly rejected by Stan as "Too dull." Amelia and Catherine scurried off in the direction of the kitchen to start the coffee, pour the juice, and warm the rolls, but before reaching their destination, the doorbell rang.

Now, my heart instantly swelled in anticipation, as I thought, "This will be Aunt Connie, come to join the fun!" but upon the front door opening, I saw it was, instead, Brittany and her husband, Gary, and their son, Michael.

The plan was thus made clear: All the girl cousins were permitted to spend Christmas Eve together, and, in aid of this arrangement, Catherine and her husband spent the night at Aunt Amelia's in the spare bedroom on the second floor. Thus Hope and Charity could sleep-over with Cynthia in her bedroom (and I use the word "sleep" in its most loose and permissive sense; as Hope, Charity and Cynthia got precious little actual "sleep," but did all expectantly occupy the same bed that night). Michael (being a boy) he could not join them, but had to sleep in his own bed, and then suffer the shock of being torn mercilessly from his warn covers before dawn to be transported in a cold car over to Aunt Amelia's, where Christmas morning waited.

Michael's arrival at ground zero was a bit different from his sisters. He rushed up to his stocking (prominently bearing his name) and began to gently, tentatively pull on it, increasing ever-so-slowly the force he applied, and clearly apprehensive that it should suddenly give way (such that an untutored observer might have questioned his self-confident manliness). However, those of us who knew him, knew the truth. Michael was previously acquainted with Aunt Amelia, and having formed—as a result of certain unfortunate and unforeseeable events (proving that "the good china" did not get its name by virtuously refusing to chip or shatter)—a not altogether benign impression of his aunt's character, he was determined to get his stocking down without incurring the wrath of "Officer Amelia" (as he secretly called her).

But the anxieties of a young boy are as a snowflake (albeit a rugged, manly snowflake) in that blizzard which characterizes the Christmas morn-

ing frenzy. Mark—being the male half of the host couple (and seeking to soften his spouse's legendary reputation for bossiness)—stood up and declared the rules: Youngest goes first, and no one can start opening the next present until the previous present has been well and truly opened— and the giver appropriately acknowledged. Also, any adult is empowered to declare a "time-out" in the event of coffee being cold, and a fresh pot needing to be started (but, tellingly, no provision was made for any time-out on account of bathroom break—this was considered not "reason-enough," and you were expected to just run and get this done between presents).

I watched all of these developments with increasing amusement— and ever-more intensifying recognition. How like this morning was to those old Christmas mornings of Molly and my doing! The girls were now older, have spouses, and have populated the day with their own offspring, showing faces, voices and habits clearly handed down from "mom." Presents got opened in the same, unexplainable ways (as if ceremonially passing down from mother to daughter the same annoyingly slow—and unfathomably pointless and obscure—rituals for removing a gift from its wrapping).

All of this I greatly enjoyed, but I did not yet see Connie. I looked up at the clock and in so doing noticed that dawn had come and gone some time ago. There having been multiple "rounds" of openings (from youngest to oldest and back to youngest several times), the number of unopened presents was dwindling. I began to be concerned. I turned to my guide and asked, "Where is Connie? She should have been here by now."

"Well, you see," he replied, "she's not here. I will tell you she's not home sick, or out of town, or nursing any sort of snit that prevents her from being here. She's just … not here."

I began to get a sick feeling in my stomach. "OK," I demanded. "I can see she's not here, so the question is, 'Why is she not here?'" I did not like the expression on my guide's face. Despite his appearance having none of that aura of mockery which so characterized Stan's demeanor, he showed on this face the same blank stare which I had seen in Stan. My guide finally answered, "She wasn't invited."

A Shock

I felt the skin of my face begin to flush, and I got hot. I had one of those brief mental seizures in which my field of vision narrowed to a point, my hearing developed an echo (as if I were imprisoned at the bottom of a deep well) and the skin of my hands felt clammy (as if my heart—in confusion—forgot to pump). "Not invited," I repeated to myself. How could I have gone from the warmest of close, familial celebrations … to this arid desert of desperation and despair? Being in the one place, how could I have known there was any risk of finding myself in the other?

As my mind struggled to make sense of what my guide had said, I gradually became aware, again, of my surroundings. Now, however, this living room given over to holiday festivities no longer offered to me any childishly joyous pastimes (no longer any presents destined to be remembered fondly, notwithstanding they were already broken). I could not bear to be exposed to any more of this hollow performance. "Not invited," I repeated to myself. My guide seeing what needed to be done, he waved his hand, and we were transported—not to the coffee shop, but to that bridge crossing over the little stream that ran very near (but outside) the boundary of the Village.

My legs would not hold me, so I jumped up to sit on the parapet, my lower legs just long enough to reach the floor of the bridge. I braced myself with both arms on the wide, comfortable stonework, and looked around distractedly. I had to try to understand what had happened. This was ... altogether unexpected, even "impossible," I finally decided. Remembering where Stan had taken me, I found a straw, and grasped it.

"This cannot be happening!" I exclaimed. "Stan took me to see my three daughters assembling pages for a photo album. Those pages were intended for Connie, and I am sure they got mailed to Connie. What is more, I saw Amelia drafting up a newsletter with Connie's name right at the top (!), and I have to believe she was sent a copy. So ... how could those same daughters, who worked so hard on those tasks (which were plainly designed to fulfill their promise to me), then turn around and not invite Connie to their Christmas morning?"

"Wait!" I shouted! "Wait, I know what happened! Stan lied to me! It can't be anything else! Oh, how foolish, how unlucky I am to have trusted him! Please!" I implored my guide, "Take away the play-acting! Show me only the truth! How could I have put myself into the hands of that ... Prince of Lies (!), who tells only so much 'truth' (the rest being falsehood) that hurt and harm and heartbreak are the only sure result?"

But my guide only retained his blankest stare and said, "No, nothing Stan showed you was false; nor was it any ambiguous mixture of truth and lies, by which deceptive truth (or accommodating lies) might tempt you away from what is real. No, Stan did not lie to you—about these things."

The Sisters Gather

That moment, I found within myself some tinge of anger; not a frequent visitor to my little, one-man, retail dispensary of legal advice, but also not one who was altogether unfamiliar to me. I gave back to my guide that "blankest stare" with which he had so recently disguised from me his inner judge-and-jury, and I made that demand of him which I had so often made of my clients: "Tell me what happened, and don't leave anything out."

My guide evinced some slight eagerness to proceed, as if he did not relish standing motionless in this position of having bad news to share, and no very convenient way to break into the conversation to deliver it. Accordingly, he once again waved his hand, and we were (per usual) instantly transported to our destination. It was another suburban kitchen, similar to the kitchens I had recently visited in the homes of Brittany and Catherine. Looking around, I saw photos on the front of the refrigerator, and quickly noting multiple well-exposed, well-focused and nicely-composed images of Cynthia, I gathered this was Amelia's kitchen.

Again, we arrived only seconds before the arrival of those whom it was intended we would eavesdrop on. These persons (Amelia, Brittany and Catherine) came in and took their seats. It was apparent I had arrived several busy hours after the moment when I had been taken away from that earlier scene of Christmas celebration. My daughters gave every appearance of being frazzled as a result of all the holiday cheer, and they now gave off that glow of quiet satisfaction arising from having at last put their respective children down for naps. Their spouses had gone off to the TV room to watch a game. Accordingly, these sisters now had some

well-earned quiet time coming to them, which they evidently had decided to fill with coffee, coffee-cake, and gossip.

I was patient as they performed a sort of "mothers' post mortem" on the morning's gift-exchange. They discussed presents of which much had been expected (but which delivered little), presents they considered only "filler" (but which turned out to be a "treasure" under the tree), and presents they had been happy to give—and which were happily received—but which could now be purchased at the local mall at sixty percent (!) off. There was much sympathy for those sisters whose most costly presents fell into this last category.

At last, they gave up discussing the events of the morning and moved on to that subject which I wished to hear. There was a considerable lull in the conversation, and then Catherine spoke up, as follows: "Do any of you feel bad about not inviting Aunt Connie? I can't help thinking about her this morning." Then she stopped. Her sisters did not rush to reply. They hesitated, as if considering how they felt about this revelation—and what to say in response. At last, Brittany allowed, "Well, if she were a regular member of the family, and we saw her any other time of the year, I would feel bad that way, but she isn't, so I don't."

Amelia jumped in, "You remember, this is not just some ordinary family get-together. This is Christmas, and I can't help remembering this is what Daddy made us promise. Still, I don't really think she could have been here."

"Yes," Brittany interjected forcefully. "There is no way Gary would accept Connie being around. He's so protective of Michael. He wouldn't want somebody ... you know, like Connie, being around his son. He's made comments before about people like her, so I'm not going to get into an argument with him on the subject. Michael is his son, and he's the father, so he wants Michael to be just as much a man as he is. So, I couldn't have Connie over, even if I wanted."

Then Catherine made her opinion known. "I don't think Alex, himself, would have any issues with Connie. Alex has a cousin who is gay—who was a friend of his since childhood—so he's not prejudiced against people like Connie. However … he does have a problem: He would not want Connie around when Hope or Charity have any of their friends over to the house. I mean … it's bound to happen that one of their parents comes over to drop them off or pick them up—and sees Connie. He says, a lot of people weren't nice to his gay cousin, and he doesn't want Hope or Charity to lose any friends—or have any of the parents of those friends decide they can't come over to play—because they see Connie at our house. But, if it were up to me, I like Connie, and I would have her over, but, you know, with us having our girls, that's just not possible."

Finally, Amelia was ready to express her views on the subject, and—being accustomed to being deferred to—she sat up a little straighter when she read out her opinion. "Look, she is, after all, our aunt. Yes, we have some history with her, and Daddy liked her, but really, she's just Daddy's younger sister. She's not my sister, so … naturally, when I have Christmas, I have it with my sisters, not necessarily with *Daddy's* sister."

Amelia continued, "She has had her whole life to find a partner, and have her own family. She has her own friends—I suppose—but we don't know any of those people, and no one would expect us to invite any of those people over here. Why, who knows what kind of people Connie has for friends? You said Alex has a gay cousin, so where does he go for Christmas? And Connie's friends—who are like Connie—where do they go for Christmas? Well, let them all go to the same place! And decrease the … 'surplus population' at those crowded Christmas parties which the rest of us attend!"

A Lesson in Contract Law

For some few moments, it looked as if this would be the final verdict on Connie's Christmas, but there was more to come. Amelia looked around and announced, "And I want to say some things about this promise which we all made to Daddy."

Her sisters got very quiet, as they could tell Amelia was about to lecture them upon some point-of-law which they knew (from bitter experience) Amelia would expect them to hear, understand and repeat-at-will should she question them on the topic in the future.

"A promise," she began, "is a contract. And a contract is—simply—this: 'I agree to do something (for you) that I would not otherwise do, and you, in return, agree to do something (for me) which you would not otherwise do.' This is basic contract law, and you can be sure Daddy understood it better, even, than I do." (Though her facial expression testified, "No, I know it better.").

"And," Amelia continued, "why is a 'contract'—or 'bargain'—such a powerful thing?" she asked, rhetorically. "It is for this reason: Because every bargain is founded upon a threat."

Amelia paused, lifting to her lips the cup of hot chocolate which sat before her, and, finishing the cup (her second), she went on.

"If I may be permitted, I would like to dramatize this part of my lesson." Her sisters made no objection (not for nothing had they known her from childhood), and—hearing no objection—Amelia started in.

"Now, imagine you have entered into just such a bargain as I have described. Imagine you did so of your own free will, not compelled to do so by any force or violence, nor so overborne by necessity that declining the bargain would have endangered your life or the life of any other person. Then, the bargain having been sealed with all solemnity, your counter-party drops his mask and speaks the following words which (undisguised by any pleasant sophistry) declare their truth in language shameless of the naked threat they make:

'Listen! You must do as I say! Not any other thing which you desire … but what I want! Have I not purchased your performance? Have you not bound yourself in fear? That seeing what you bargained-for at risk of loss, you steel yourself to do that thing which I am owed.'

'Obey me, then! I do not give you leave, in this, to seek your pleasure; nor will I suffer your delay, defiance or regret.'

'I warn you, now! If you debase yourself so much that you repudiate your solemn promise, then I shall act! In such a case … standing blameless before the world … innocent of any injury which you may thereby suffer, I shall declare our sacred bargain 'void.'''

Having performed the foregoing scene, Amelia now spoke directly to her audience. "And so we see is every contract subject to being 'broken.' And when we say 'broken,' do we not imply that some force or violence has been used? And this pursuant to a 'threat'? "

(Now, every great dramatic performance concludes with one, climactic soliloquy, ensuring that the audience—though dazzled by the dramatist's art, and mesmerized by the actor's talent—will nevertheless get the point). Here was Amelia's:

"Thus you see ... is every bargain founded upon a threat, and bounded 'round by vigilance (that I will watch to see if you comply), and written out in many words in judgment (that nothing might be changed, avoided or declined). So says the law.

And I—its servant—testify to this, as well, a warning you do well to heed:

You! Who would knit together a world out of bonds of love and loyalty, must taste despair, for love is fickle and loyalty no stronger than the perishable will of man.

The law, however, being constructed of inflexible rules ... fastened together with unalterable words, and built upon a foundation of unyielding principle, will sooner break the back of those who trust in love and loyalty, than give an inch in answer to your plea in mitigation."

(The curtain having come down on her impromptu drama, Amelia decided she would leave to others the job of commenting upon her stagecraft, and the over-all artistic mood created by her performance.)

Finally (lawyers never knowing when they ought to just sit down and shut up), Amelia amended her lecture by adding the following words:

"We lawyers are taught that every contract comes into existence only in accordance with the 'law,' and, the law being transparent to our reason (however opaque it may be to our hearts), there is nothing that will hide the nature of the threat. For when we speak of the 'Majesty of the Law,' do we not sometimes forget that 'Majesty' is a word denoting 'King?' And a 'King' a person possessing so much unfettered power that, between the threat (he makes) and the imprisonment or death (you suffer), there is only so much whimsy as suits his idle pleasure."

Advice of Counsel

Having finished her lecture, Amelia went on with her comments, "Now, for several years I have had no problem living up to our little contract with Daddy, but recently, I decided that there were good reasons why I shouldn't have to, so I have decided that, in the future, I am not going to do so. And here is the first reason I have made this decision."

"Though he obtained our promise that we would do something 'we would not otherwise do,' he did not—in return—agree to do anything for us! No, he simply expected us to keep our end of the bargain 'out of the goodness of our hearts.' But, (speaking-up for myself, as I must) the 'goodness of my heart' is not to be purchased so cheaply. Why, what benefit do I derive from this bargain? What claim could Daddy (or, for that matter, Aunt Connie) possibly have upon my 'goodness' that I would be compelled to recognize this unequal bargain?"

"Now, if Daddy had been honest and acknowledged from the beginning that he was merely soliciting a kind of 'gift' from each of us (that gathered, grateful 'goodness of our hearts'), I might have been willing to make some charitable gesture in response. But, in the case of a bargain where it is self-evident that I will receive nothing of pecuniary value in return, I cannot help but feel that (already being found 'blameless'), there is nothing more required of me."

"And, in final summation ... " (Amelia—having so recently made an elaborate speech upon one of the finer points of contract law—seemed to have forgotten she was not in court). "Whatever 'goodness' Daddy may have expected of me in this case ('goodness' being a virtue which, while laudatory, has never been known to satisfy any earthly bargain), it is, after all, something which I am free to disregard, as neither he nor anyone else in this world has any power over me, to enforce such a bargain."

Amelia paused to let her listeners catch their breath. Catherine and Brittany, meanwhile, sat perfectly motionless, seeming to fear that any movement on their part might attract unwelcome attention (as if a rabbit, sitting motionless in the tall weeds, and feigning an intense and all-consuming interest in the law's definition of "consideration," might depend for its continued survival upon other, even more distracting elements of contract law, in which the fox is very much absorbed.)

"Next, when Daddy asked, for example, you, Brittany, to keep Aunt Connie as part of your family, and to have her over to visit from time to time, and to have her here at Christmastime, Daddy was, actually, asking you to promise to do something 'impossible!' (And, as you can easily guess, no court will force any party to a contract to do anything which is 'impossible.')"

"And what Daddy asked is 'impossible,' because Gary would forbid it! He would say 'No.' And you can't go against your husband, and do something he objects to. I mean ... what kind of wife would you be if you disobeyed him ... after he gave you his 'final decision' (which is not open to debate) that Connie was not to be invited to your house, where Michael might see her? So, probably what Daddy really meant was that you should 'try' to have Aunt Connie over, but only if no one objects, and only if no one would be embarrassed or made uncomfortable being around her."

Finally, Amelia said, "Here is the third reason I have decided *not* to follow this promise any more: You remember, I said a contract is when one person requires the other person to do something 'she would not otherwise do.' Well ... you see! Daddy knew that having Aunt Connie around is something that none of us 'would otherwise do!' He knew that—without the promise—none of us would keep Connie in our family. It wouldn't make sense! I mean ... what advantage would there be in that for us?"

Going on, Amelia leaned forward and lowered her voice, as if whispering news of some heretofore secret crime of which their father had been guilty, which, by revealing it, she thereby initiated them into an equally mysterious conspiracy to keep the "secret" of that guilty fault. "What makes me a little angry," (Amelia had mastered that lawyer's trick of resorting to "Anger, on Account of Self-Evident Injustice" when her argument got a little thin), "is that Daddy would even ask us to do something like this! Something he knew we 'wouldn't ordinarily do,' and *certainly* wouldn't do, if we were to do what he always taught us to do, which was to think for ourselves, and not let anyone else tell us how to live our lives!"

The Final Verdict

Amelia's sisters sat unresponsive, each passively allowing this caustic, scalding shower of antipathy (poured out by their sister) to silently soak in, but also tentatively waiting out the deluge, to see if there was any moisture yet remaining in those storm clouds (which, if so, they needed to sit quietly under cover). However, as the moments passed, and Brittany and Catherine could see the clouds abating, they ventured out into the conversation again, and seeking some fresh and temperate comments to make (in helpful acknowledgement of the downpour), at last spoke up.

Brittany began. "Actually, yesterday, I was speaking to Gary, you know, when we were getting ready to go to church, and I brought up the subject of Connie. I suggested to him that we could invite Connie to go with us to the service, and maybe sit with us, and that we could spend a little time with her, you know, maybe after the service, in the parlor where the minister always has coffee."

"He told me that he hoped no one would see Connie with us in the church, because she was 'unnatural,' and it might be unpleasant to them to be reminded upon Christmas Day, of those lame, defective people, who any blind man can see have something 'wrong.'"

Now that Brittany had bared her heart, it was Catherine's turn. "Well, to tell you the truth, recently I was thinking about Aunt Connie, and I almost let her meet Hope and Charity. You know, I like to take them over to the roller rink, to go rollerblading with their friends, and we often stop off for pizza on the way (like Connie used to do with us) so their friends can meet us there, and we can all go out to the rink together in one car."

"I was thinking, you know, that Connie could get pizza with us, and then go out to the rink and watch all the girls skate, like we used to do. Not that Connie would be skating—I expect she's too old for that—but there's no reason she couldn't be there to sit in the snack bar, and watch all the kids skate, and tighten everybody's laces like she used to do."

"But then, I started thinking about my daughters' friends, and the parents of those friends. Most of them are professional people—lawyers and accountants and brokers and stuff like that. And you know, those people, they are just so 'single-minded.' They don't want to do anything that might put their kids at risk, and I was just afraid they would, you know, object to Connie (not that they know her, or have any reason to be concerned, but just 'on principle,' you know). It's like you said, Amelia. If she has her own friends, or anybody she could call 'family,' then she should be with them, and if she doesn't have any friends, or family, then that's just 'nature's way' of dealing with people like Connie, and who are we to judge?"

"Then we are all agreed," Amelia summed up. "We agree that Daddy's bargain is a false one, and as to us: 'invalid.' As to any other people (meaning, in this case, our husbands and children), they are not parties to this fraudulent contract, and we must leave them out of it."

But Catherine, still having in her mind a vivid picture of Hope and Charity doing the Hokey-Pokey, she did not want to drop the question, but had more to say. "I do not feel comfortable doing 'nothing.' I can't just drop everything and leave her out entirely."

Catherine spoke with emotion. "When I think about Aunt Connie, I have a lot of fond memories of things we did—we all did—and favors she did for us. I agree there's no way she can be a part of our lives going forward (husbands and kids and friends and all that 'family' stuff), but we can still remember all those times we had *before* Daddy made us promise. If I just leave out all these other people, there is still the three of us and Mother and Daddy. I can still remember those times—on Christmas Day."

So saying, the girls prepared to decide how they might satisfy their sentimental sister, while at the same time transitioning to that entirely voluntary (and thereby wholly unenforceable) arrangement which they had been advised (by counsel) to implement.

My guide seeing in me no longer any heart to listen, nor any wishes yet unspoiled, he waved his hand, and so took me away from that cold and sterile place.

A Christmas Spectre

I stood on the bridge, leaning on the parapet and looking over the edge at the water flowing determinedly downstream. This stream, I saw, behaved as if it believed obeying the law of gravity (seeking its own level) was some hydrological virtue of which it might pride itself (when called upon to give account). But, however much virtue I might see in so lowly a thing as this gentle stream (as if so many tears collected, some part of me recalled), there was—this moment—no other virtue I could find in life.

I shifted my hands on the stonework and suddenly felt the sharpest pain in my thumb! I jerked my hands back in shock! My guide looked at me pityingly and explained, "No doubt you pricked yourself on one of those 'serpent's teeth' of which we have all read so much, and dread to encounter. You will be lucky if you suffer only this one injury (attributable only to the one tooth), yours being a case in which my knowledge of herpetology (and genealogy) suggests the (hidden) presence of two other, additional teeth which are likewise to be feared."

Presently, my guide brought me back to where we had left off. He said, "We have completed your time with the Ghost of Christmas Past, and the Ghost of Christmas Present Day. Now you must place yourself in the hands of the Ghost of Christmas Yet to Come and see what he will show you. This is required."

So saying, he waved his hand, and his appearance instantly changed. He now stood before me wearing that long, black, hooded robe which we invariably associate with Death and Doom and Tragic Fate. I saw, however, my guide's kindly face showing out from beneath the hood of that mysterious garment, and thus, where others might have felt themselves in the presence of "Concealed, Implacable Evil," I saw only "Pre-Shrunk Polyester Blend."

My guide did not give me any more time to ponder. Again he waved his hand, and we were transported to a scene I had never seen before. We were standing in the corner of a small living room—in the dark, shortly before dawn. I could not make out much in the darkness, but did sense the presence of another person. Suddenly, the lights on a small, table-top Christmas tree came on, providing colorful and cheery illumination enough to look around the room.

Then! I saw Connie! She was standing over by the wall, where she had just plugged in the lights on the tree. I watched as she walked (unsteadily) a few paces to a chair opposite the tree. She looked much as I remembered her, though older, grayer, less lively, and obviously grateful to take her seat. Otherwise, she appeared to be the same gentle soul I had known. She wore a long, threadbare robe (we might mistake it for

"brand new" if "Faded Frayed Fancy Faux Fur" were a desirable material from which to construct a bathrobe), slippers (run down at the heels), and her hair pulled back into a pony-tail to deep it from falling into her eyes.

At last seeing her, I eagerly looked from her face to her robe to her feet, trying to see if there had been any considerable change in her appearance—which there was not. I studied her intently, thinking that she would soon begin moving about the room, initiating those activities which are so characteristic of a Christmas morning. But ... nothing changed. She sat motionless before the tree, as if lost in some private thoughts which even I, her brother, closest to her in age and blood and flesh, could not divine.

Without giving any warning, my guide waved his hand in my direction. I did not grasp the import of this gesture until, seconds later, Connie called out, "Oh! Tommy! It's you, Tommy!" Her face lit up, bright with joy and surprise. She smiled her kindest smile, and leaned forward ever so slightly (testimony to her glasses being still in the other room). She said no more, only gazing at my image in happy wonderment, drinking in that vision of her older brother, who had so many times been a comfort to her.

For my part, I was stupefied. I knew my guide had done something bold, breaking every rule. I did not know whether to speak to him (asking what was permitted to me) or whether it were better to seize the moment, and speak to Connie. Then, I decided that if I could speak, I would, and give my sister whatever encouragement I could. However, it soon became apparent to me that I was to be prevented from speaking— or from moving about the room in any way. I did have the power, at least, to smile at her, and show her in my face how much I loved her, and missed her, and would many more times come back from the grave (if so much is required) to keep her safe and happy.

I tried and found that I was free to move my arms, which I promptly did, holding out my hands to her as if in blessing, and acting out (in silent show of my affection) my mute bestowal of mercy and forgiveness.

Then once more Connie found her voice. "Oh, Tommy. I was just sitting here, thinking about one of the Christmases I had at your house— yours and Molly's. I remember it was early—like this, before dawn—and I was staying in the spare bedroom at your house, and then, I came downstairs and turned on the tree—like this one." She motioned toward her tree. "And I was thinking ... dreaming, really, about 'what if this tree were mine?' What if … I was like a normal woman, and had a husband, and children—still sleeping upstairs. And that was my tree! And sitting here, if anyone were to see me, they wouldn't know it wasn't my tree, and there was no husband and no children upstairs, and there never would be those things, no matter how much I wished them to be."

She reached up and dabbed away a tear. "So … I'm sorry, Tommy. I know it wasn't right. It wasn't my tree. It was yours … and Molly's and the girls'. It wasn't right for me to wish it away from you, and dream it for myself. I'm not a person who has those things, like trees with presents all around, or little girls who make a mess of morning, or stockings filled with candy, toys and tangerines. Please forgive me, Tommy. Those things were yours … and Molly's. This tree I keep to remember you … and if I had not been so selfish, and wanted all those things for myself, maybe my life would have turned out different; maybe someone would have wanted me … someone as kind as you, Tommy."

My guide had not permitted me to speak or move … but nothing in his power could forestall my tears, which—appearing on my cheek—I could see that Connie noticed them, and moved as if to stand and come to me, to dry them with the sleeve of her robe. But doing so, she broke the spell (my guide compelled to intervene), and with the wave of a hand I lost my darling sister, my image lost to her for ever more.

Connie's Family Album

But despite this tender moment, so apropos of parting, we did not go. My guide did not wave either of his hands (keeping them soldierly against his body in rigid truculence). Connie sat for some little while after my departure, as if storing away bits and scraps and end-pieces out of the fabric of this precious reunion (whereof she might use them again someday, if she determines to piece together another wistful dream in which her brotherly protector appears).

Finally, Connie stood up and, sighing, went into her kitchen to fix a cup of hot chocolate (so satisfying to her on a cold Christmas morning). Then I saw her take her cup and go into her modest dining room and, setting the cup down where she could reach it, she went to an open cabinet back in the living room. There she retrieved several home-made, self-decorated photo albums (constructed of materials obtained by Connie at the local craft supplies store), and bringing them back to the dining room, she set them down beside her cup. Next, being seated, she picked one out and opened it.

Now, I was exceedingly anxious to look over her shoulder and see what she saw in those albums. However, my experience with Stan made me think that I would not be permitted to stand so close to her as to be able to peek over her shoulder (which, in my present ghostly state, I felt sure would not annoy her, whereas any living kibitzer would be instantly shoed-away). Nevertheless, my guide sensing my hesitancy, he reached over and gave me a little shove in her direction, and I was soon standing where I could readily see and read everything on the table before her.

Connie took a sip of hot chocolate and began. She opened the first album to the first page and methodically worked her way through to the end. Now, I did not have access to her thoughts, and what I say (I admit) is merely my uninformed impression, but it seemed to me she had paged through this album many, many times before.

Watching the pages flipping over, I was pleased to see many photos well-known to me—both as photos (to be seen and loved again) and as memories (I having been the photographer). There were photos from those years when the girls were young, and only slowly growing up. There were shots of birthday parties, vacations, holidays (among them, Christmas) and other random photos immortalizing pets (including gerbils, fish and the occasional rabbit), but in all cases featuring each and all of the girls, singly or in combination with their mother and (but rarely) me.

Her hot chocolate being no longer "hot," Connie paused to go back to the kitchen and pour herself a fresh and warmed-up cup. Coming back, she resumed turning the pages, and I continued to reminisce ... except that, I began to be a little puzzled. Something seemed odd. Then it hit me! There were no photos of Connie! And I know this was not just a re-flection of the subject matter—where the photographer could not have included Connie in a photo of an event she had not attended. No! Here were Christmas mornings where I knew (!) she had been present. I saw the evidence! Catherine, smiling in her pajamas, holding up her new rollerblades. Amelia, looking shy and uncomfortable before the camera, the pointe shoes nestled on her lap.

Yes! Where was Connie in these photos? Someone had put together these pages and sent them to Connie (for her album), but on no page was there any image of Aunt Connie, no matter how prominent she had been at that place and time. That earlier feeling I had had—that sick feeling in my stomach—started to come back.

Connie finished the first album, which in the end I saw went only up to that year and time when the last daughter (Brittany) moved out of the house. After that, there were no more pages. Upon consideration, this made some sense to me, as Connie had three more albums to page through. Still, I could not understand how anyone—knowing our family—could have portrayed its history (photographically) without featuring multiple pictures of Connie (for whom the Chicken Dance was both "choreographic art" and "low-impact cardio workout").

Connie's Christmas Gifts

The next album which Connie pulled down in front of her was likewise rich with candid family photos. Almost at once, I realized which pages these were. At the top of each page was the name of one of the sisters, and below it on that page were multiple candid, "newsy" photos of that daughter. This album, I could see, was given over to those pages edited and assembled by Catherine. I had watched her make these pages (at least, those for the current year) and here they were, bound and collected.

But once again, I developed an uneasy feeling about the pages, and with only a little consideration I realized what the problem was. There were, for example, on those pages headed "Catherine," photos of her in multiple different places and times ... but nowhere in those photos did I see any appearance of her husband, Alex, or—worse—of Hope or Charity. Connie turned to pages identified "Amelia," and saw pictorial evidence of her achievements. But nowhere did I see any accomplishments of Cynthia, nor any photos of Amelia (and Mark) hugging Cynthia close in loving family portraits.

There were no children in this album! No children, and no husbands! Just my girls—"grown up." Grown-up and working, grown-up and shopping, grown-up and cooking. And, to show that creativity was not lack-

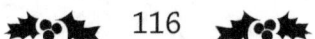

ing, I saw here and there shots of "Amelia gardening with Catherine," or "Brittany shopping with Amelia." Yes, they were not shy about showing themselves the "social butterfly," even going so far as to appear together (in every permutation of the "3") within the same flutter of like-minded butterflies—providing such photos revealed no "butterfly spouse" or "butterfly child."

I looked—stricken—at my guide. He did not speak, but only pointed in the direction of the next album, which Connie now opened to the front. These, I saw (I was expecting this), were the pages collected, edited and drawn out by Brittany. These were the pages each headed with one of those tiny little 'school photos' so well-designed for trading. I leaned over Connie's shoulder to better see these photos, and doing so, I nearly gasped in shock! I was at first confused. Something terrible had occurred! Something impossible had happened!

The photos at the top of each page did not in any case correspond to the child whose name was written there! I saw one page entitled "Michael," but the photo was not Brittany's son, but some other young man (of comparable age) having similar hair color and general facial resemblance to Michael. Of the page entitled "Charity," there was a tiny little photo of another girl (not Catherine's daughter), and below that photo on the same page were a variety of photos of that same young girl (a stranger) obviously printed off some photo-sharing website. These were Brittany's pages! She assembled these, using the photos supplied by her sisters (and some contributed by herself), and none of them showed that true and honest face of the child it claimed to portray!

I saw these pages now for what they were. Each sister had gone into that little stack of tiny photos collected by her son or daughter and picked out one that more-or-less resembled her own child (if you kind of squinted, and looked at it from the side, in the right kind of light). Then sending these to their sister, Brittany downloaded photographic 'filler' from a photo-sharing website used by that child, and pasted the pages together in easy satisfaction of her (voluntary, in no way obligatory) assignment. Thus, I saw that in these pages, Brittany had for Connie no "Cynthia," no "Michael," no "Hope," and (you saw this coming) no "Charity."

There was no doubt what my daughters had agreed. There were to be photos of themselves—even current, candid and honest photos showing them in the midst of life. They would hold nothing back, nor hide themselves: Their work, their daily chores, their amusements. But what they would not show is this: Their husbands or their children.

As it was so very ably explained by counsel: These people were not parties to the bargain; they must be hidden from Connie; she has no enforceable right to see them.

There was, I knew, one final album yet to be reviewed. Connie slid it over in front of her, opened it, and commenced reading. Each page I could see was a page of that "Newsletter" having a circulation of "one." Here, I thought, the girls could not help but abandon their relentless fixation on excluding husbands and children. (As where else would you find the "news" but in that active, lively younger generation?) But once again, I had underestimated my eldest daughter. Where other lawyers might excel in evaluating a case, and giving advice (as did Amelia), there were few who had her talent for clever and inventive drafting.

The newsletter (I had seen before) was divided according to the month, and each month reported events and activities native to that month. How-

ever, now reading what Amelia had written, I saw her purpose, and how she played her game.

For February, for example, she wrote, "Brittany had car trouble, and had to get her water pump replaced." Then, for March, she wrote, "Catherine signed up for a cooking class, where she will learn how to bake pastries for Easter." Then equally revelatory, for herself (for April), she wrote, "Amelia collected all her financial documents, filling two big banker's boxes, and dropped them off at her accountant's office." This noteworthy, revealing, and profoundly personal entry was immediately followed by another, of equal emotional intensity: "Then later, Amelia got her tax return back from the accountant, signed it, and mailed it in."

Thus entirely defeated, I could only marvel at Amelia's triumphantly clever plan. She told news only regarding herself and her sisters, and never referred in any way to any husbands or children. She told only so much news as might reveal no more than the most trivial, routine and commonplace activities of herself and her siblings, never including any mention of anything private or personal.

And last, she told only so much of the "news" as would unfailingly demonstrate that Amelia (and her sisters) were at all times successful in their struggles with the vicissitudes of life (never suffering any failures, illnesses or losses worth mentioning). She scrupulously refrained from reporting any "news" which (being read by Connie), might inflame her aunt's passionate anxiety for the welfare of her nieces, and thereby induce Connie to reach out to the afflicted sister (in the stead of her departed brother) to offer her assistance.

Thus, never knowing of any ill-events befalling any of the sisters, Connie was kept in blissful ignorance. According to this plan, Amelia was assured that neither she nor any of her siblings would suffer any unwanted expression of love or sympathy bestowed upon them by their aunt. (Connie having such tender emotions, everyone knew she was more than ordinarily susceptible to their sudden, sympathetic agitation, whereas Amelia—being a lawyer—knew many ways of smothering Sympathy in its crib.)

My ghostly tour was ended. All secrets were revealed. My grief is this: That my daughters, although unwilling to live up to the terms of the bargain they had made (electing, instead, to proffer only "partial performance" in mitigation of their default), did at the same time hold the Majesty of the Law in such superstitious awe that they could not bring themselves to altogether repudiate their obligations under that agreement. Alas, being thereby disinclined either to honor the law or to break it, they now so devoted themselves to empty ritual (devoid of any efficacious purpose) that Connie—visiting the snack bar at the roller rink, and tapping her foot in time to the Hokey Pokey, and seeing the skaters "shake it all about"—might have smiled at any of their children ... without recognizing them.

The silence was profound. I could not speak, nor find within myself sufficient anger to challenge what I had seen. This was, after all, no longer my world. Hereafter, the only role open to me is to be that perfect observer: standing silent, observing all, and bearing eternal witness to what I have seen.

I saw that Connie had finished flipping through her final album—and had likewise finished her final cup of chocolate. I saw her stand and take her cup into the kitchen. There, she put her cup into the sink and changed over to drinking that fizzy Italian lemonade, which she liked so much. Finally, she went back into the dining room, picked up her albums, and took them into the living room, where she put them safely away.

The albums, I saw, were much like Connie, each having a cover poor and worn and mended, but brave in ribbons.

About the Author

The author, Holly Maholm, is a transgender woman living in Cleveland, Ohio. For most of her life, Holly lived as a man, but in 2013 she began her transition to living as a woman. Since coming out, Holly has been active in the Cleveland transgender community. Holly has been married twice and has three grown daughters, from her first marriage. Any similarity between the author's daughters and any character in this book is purely coincidental. Holly is also the author—under her prior, male name—of a book *When Once I Lived* (Angry Rabbit Enterprises, 2011) which prominently features several of the same characters met with in this book.

www.ingramcontent.com/pod-product-compliance
Lightning Source LLC
Chambersburg PA
CBHW081154170626

46813CB00009B/3191